San Jose
Clara
Merced
Merced
Madera
Madera
Santa Cruz
Santa Cruz
Gilroy
Big Pine
KINGS CANYON NP
KINGS CANYON NP
Inyo
Salinas
Fresno
Fresno
Mt Whitney 14,494'
DEATH VALLEY NP
Monterey
San Benito
Selma
Squaw Valley
SEQUOIA NP
PINNACLES NP
Panamint Springs
Hanford
Visalia
Death Valley Junction
Big Sur
King City
Tulare
Tulare
Olancha
San Lucas
Kings
Monterey
Kettleman City
Shoshone
Delano
San Simeon
Paso Robles
Ridgecrest
Cambria
San Luis Obispo
Buttonwillow
Bakersfield
Morro Bay
San Luis Obispo
Mojave Desert
Kern
MOJAVE PRE
Pismo Beach
Tehachapi
Kelso
Maricopa
Wheeler Ridge
Barstow
Santa Maria
Grapevine
San Bernardino
Lancaster
Santa Barbara
Lompoc
Solvang
Palmdale
Victorville
Santa Barbara
Santa Barbara
Santa Clarita
Los Angeles
Ventura
Oxnard
Pasadena
San Bernardino
Yucca Valley
Twentynine Pa
Ontario
Rancho Cucamonga
Malibu
Los Angeles
Santa Monica
Riverside
JOSHUA TREE NP
CHANNEL ISLANDS NP
Anaheim
Palm Springs
Indio
Long Beach
Santa Ana
Riverside
Huntington Beach
Orange
Santa Catalina Island
San Clemente
Salt
PACIFIC OCEAN
Avalon
Oceanside
Escondido
San Diego
ANZA-BORREGO DESERT SP
Del Mar
La Jolla
Alpine
El Cent
San Diego
MEXICO

American Birding Association
Field Guide to Birds
of California

American Birding Association

Field Guide to Birds of California

Alvaro Jaramillo

PHOTOGRAPHS BY
Brian E. Small,
Mike Danzenbaker,
Bob Steele,
Alan Murphy,
AND OTHERS

Scott & Nix, Inc.
NEW YORK

A SCOTT & NIX EDITION

PUBLISHED BY SCOTT & NIX, INC.
150 W 28TH ST, STE 1900
NEW YORK, NY 10001
SCOTTANDNIX.COM

FIRST EDITION 2015

ISBN 978-1-935622-50-5

AMERICAN BIRDING ASSOCIATION, INC.
800-850-2473
ABA.ORG

SCOTT & NIX, INC. BOOKS
ARE DISTRIBUTED TO THE TRADE BY:

INDEPENDENT PUBLISHERS GROUP (IPG)
814 NORTH FRANKLIN STREET
CHICAGO, IL 60610
800-888-4741
IPGBOOK.COM

PRINTED IN CHINA

Contents

The American Birding Association inspires all people to enjoy and protect wild birds.

The ABA represents the North American birding community and supports birders through publications, conferences, workshops, events, partnerships, and networks.

The ABA's education programs promote birding skills, ornithological knowledge, and the development of and implementation of a conservation ethic.

The ABA encourages birders to apply their skills to help conserve birds and their habitats, and we represent the interests of birders in planning and legislative arenas.

We welcome all birders as members.

THE AMERICAN BIRDING ASSOCIATION CODE OF ETHICS

Everyone who enjoys birds and birding must always respect wildlife, its environment, and the rights of others. In any conflict of interest between birds and birders, the welfare of the birds and their environment comes first.

CODE OF BIRDING ETHICS

1. Promote the welfare of birds and their environment.

   1(a) Support the protection of important bird habitat.

   1(b) To avoid stressing birds or exposing them to danger, exercise restraint and caution during observation, photography, sound recording, or filming.

Limit the use of recordings and other methods of attracting birds, and never use such methods in heavily birded areas, or for attracting any species that is Threatened, Endangered, or of Special Concern, or is rare in your local area; Keep well back from nests and nesting colonies, roosts, display areas, and important feeding sites. In such sensitive areas, if there is a need for extended observation, photography, filming, or recording, try to use a blind or hide, and take advantage of natural cover.

Use artificial light sparingly for filming or photography, especially for close-ups.

1(c) Before advertising the presence of a rare bird, evaluate the potential for disturbance to the bird, its surroundings, and other people in the area, and proceed only if access can be controlled, disturbance minimized, and permission has been obtained from private land-owners. The sites of rare nesting birds should be divulged only to the proper conservation authorities.

1(d) Stay on roads, trails, and paths where they exist; otherwise keep habitat disturbance to a minimum.

2. Respect the law, and the rights of others.

2(a) Do not enter private property without the owner's explicit permission.

2(b) Follow all laws, rules, and regulations governing use of roads and public areas, both at home and abroad.

2(c) Practice common courtesy in contacts with other people. Your exemplary behavior will generate goodwill with birders and non-birders alike.

3. Ensure that feeders, nest structures, and other artificial bird environments are safe.

3(a) Keep dispensers, water, and food clean, and free of decay or disease. It is important to feed birds continually during harsh weather.

3(b) Maintain and clean nest structures regularly.

3(c) If you are attracting birds to an area, ensure the birds are not exposed to predation from cats and other domestic animals, or dangers posed by artificial hazards.

4. Group birding, whether organized or impromptu, requires special care.

Each individual in the group, in addition to the obligations spelled out in Items 1 and 2, has responsibilities as a Group Member.

4(a) Respect the interests, rights, and skills of fellow birders, as well as people participating in other legitimate outdoor activities. Freely share your knowledge and experience, except where code 1(c) applies. Be especially helpful to beginning birders.

4(b) If you witness unethical birding behavior, assess the situation, and intervene if you think it prudent. When interceding, inform the person(s) of the inappropriate action, and attempt, within reason, to have it stopped. If the behavior continues, document it, and notify appropriate individuals or organizations.

Group Leader Responsibilities [amateur and professional trips and tours].

4(c) Be an exemplary ethical role model for the group. Teach through word and example.

4(d) Keep groups to a size that limits impact on the environment, and does not interfere with others using the same area.

4(e) Ensure everyone in the group knows of and practices this code.

4(f) Learn and inform the group of any special circumstances applicable to the areas being visited (e.g. no tape recorders allowed).

4(g) Acknowledge that professional tour companies bear a special responsibility to place the welfare of birds and the benefits of public knowledge ahead of the company's commercial interests. Ideally, leaders should keep track of tour sightings, document unusual occurrences, and submit records to appropriate organizations.

Everyone who enjoys birds and birding must always respect wildlife, its environment, and the rights of others. The ABA Code of Ethics should be read, followed, and shared by all birders.

Please follow this code and distribute and teach it to others.

The American Birding Association's Code of Birding Ethics may be freely reproduced for distribution/dissemination. An electronic version may be found at aba.org/about/ethics.

Foreword

Congratulations! If you're reading this, it's safe to say that you're either thinking about birding in California, or you've already gotten a taste and want more. Congratulations because you've hit the jackpot. California birding is as fine and varied as its wines and as entertaining and exciting as any Hollywood movie, often more so. You're starting at the top.

This book, like all the guides in this series, can help you do whatever you want with birding. Perhaps you enjoy birds only a few days a year in your yard or local park or perhaps you want to dive deeper and get more familiar with more of the many amazing birds in the Golden State. In choosing this book, you're putting yourself in the supremely capable hands of Alvaro Jaramillo, who is as sharp a birder and as inspiring a teacher as you'll find anywhere. I've been lucky to bird with thousands of people and there's nobody who bests Alvaro when it comes to knowing his stuff, yet being able to share his vast knowledge in a way that will make you feel smarter. And you've got another supremely talented Californian in your corner. Native son Brian E. Small took the bulk of the photos here, as he does for all the ABA State Guides.

I invite you to visit the American Birding Association website (aba.org), where you'll find a wealth of free resources and ways to connect with our community that will help you get the most from your birding in California and beyond. Please consider becoming an ABA member yourself—one of the best parts of birding is joining a community of fun, passionate people.

Now get on out there! Enjoy this book. Enjoy California. And most of all, enjoy birding!

Good birding,

Jeffrey A Gordon

Jeffrey A. Gordon, *President*
American Birding Association

Birds of California

California is the third largest of the United States, ranking in total area after only Texas and Alaska. Within this enormous area are amazingly rich and diverse habitats for birds. There are high mountains, hill country, rocky and sandy coastlines, watered woodlands, bone-dry deserts, fertile valleys, and vast urban and suburban areas, all of which attract many types of birds. Indeed, California may be the most ecologically diverse state or province in the United States and Canada. That is most likely why it has the highest "bird list." The official list of birds observed and recorded in the state includes 657 bird species to date. On average, the list gains one or two species per year and is currently almost 20 species larger than Texas, the next most species-rich state. The diversity of habitats, including the many preserves and parks, along with the sheer size of California, makes it one of the best places to see birds in North America.

Some habitats are unique to, or mainly found in California, which provide homes for the state's bird specialties. These habitats include the ring of oak woodlands around the Great Central Valley, the Channel Islands, the coastal scrub of the

The Island Scrub-Jay is found only on Santa Cruz Island, part of the northern group of the Channel Islands of California.

south, and chaparral habitats farther inland, as well as the rich California offshore current. There are two bird species entirely endemic to California, the Yellow-billed Magpie and the Island Scrub-Jay. The magpie is found in the oak belt, and the Central Valley, where it shares its habitat with some other regional specialties, such as the Oak Titmouse, Nuttall's Woodpecker, and White-breasted Nuthatch. The Island Scrub-Jay on the other hand is found on Santa Cruz Island in the Channel Islands, where various unique geographic populations, called subspecies, of California birds are found, as well as some specialty seabirds, such as Black Storm-Petrel and Scripps's Murrelet. The coastal scrub and chaparral are home to the Wrentit and California Thrasher, two more specialties, as well as the California Gnatcatcher in the south and the coastal subspecies of the Cactus Wren, among others. The nutrient rich waters off California, and its massive submarine canyon in Monterey Bay, make it one of the best places to look for seabirds in the world. Birds from Mexico, the Arctic, Antarctic, Chile, New Zealand, and many distant islands in the Pacific come here to spend part of their annual life cycle. In addition, the Ashy Storm-Petrel breeds essentially only within the state.

California also shares habitats with adjacent areas, such as the temperate rain forests of the Pacific Northwest, the Great Sagebrush Desert, and the Sonoran Desert. In addition, chains of mountains along the coast, as well as the more eastern

The Wrentit's home is California's dense chaparral habitats.

Cascades and Sierras, and the Transverse and southern mountains, with their varied elevations, add habitat complexity. California is a state where Great Gray Owls and Pine Grosbeaks of the north can be found at higher elevations above sites where Phainopeplas and Lesser Goldfinches of arid southern areas are found.

California may continue to grow in its avian diversity. Some regionally restricted populations or subspecies of birds may be elevated to full species by scientists, further creating specialty birds found in California. The tendency for California to receive vagrant birds from the East, as well as from Asia, will continue to excite birders interested in fulfilling a California birding life list. California is a must stop for birders trying to learn and see the birds of North America, because there are so many unique species or habitats here that are not found elsewhere in the continent.

All of these factors and more combine to make California a fantastic place to observe and extraordinary variety of birds in their native habitats and in surprising places where they have wandered far from home.

The Varied Thrush breeds in the moist, dark forests of northwestern California.

Why Birdwatching?

Why *not* birds could be an answer, of course. But the question is really what draws so many people to birds, perhaps more than other aspects of the natural world, from whales, butterflies, dragonflies, bats, and fishes? Birds are mostly active in the day, they sing in frequencies we can hear, and enjoy, and they show off their feathered plumages in colors we can see and admire. Most mammals are reclusive, often nocturnal, or have habits that keep them from being seen easily. On the other hand, experienced birders can go to a great birding site in California in various months of the year and see over 100 species of birds in one day with just a bit of concentrated effort. You may need years and years of searching to see 100 species of mammals, or to be able to identify 100 species of small moths. Birds are abundant and nearly everywhere you seek them out. And birds are the perfect gateway to begin watching nature. They are abundant, beautiful, and in many ways, some of the easiest animals to identify. Birdwatching (often called birding) can help us learn the skills we need to then understand dragonflies or whales, or whatever other exciting creature you choose to look for!

The Costa's Hummingbird is closely associated with the desert environments of southwestern California.

Birds in This Guide

This field guide covers 308 species of birds that occur commonly in California. Many of the more than 650 species in the official California list are rarities, birds that show up once a year or maybe even less. These are often vagrant or "lost" birds that visit briefly instead of the regular and annual visitors to the state. As such, the birds chosen for this book are a subset of all the birds of California. These are the ones birders, particularly beginning birders, are likely to find in their region with some regularity. Some less common species are included in this guide: they may be uncommon, but are seen annually in California. Several "pelagic" species, those which are seen only offshore or not too far from shore, are included. As California is a state where one of its specialty habitats is the Pacific California current, it is important to include a sampling of offshore birds. These birds may be seen by taking a special pelagic birding trip on a boat, or perhaps during a whale-watching excursion.

The order of species in the guide is arranged taxonomically as set forth by scientists. This order, which begins with older evolutionary lineages of birds and ends with the types of birds considered more modern, groups birds that are most closely related. This book largely follows this scientific order with some minor deviations to organize some very similar looking species next to each other for better comparison. Understanding how groups of birds are related to one another can greatly aid in the identification and enjoyment of birding.

Species Accounts

Each species account gives the official English and scientific name of the bird as determined by the *Check-list* of the American Ornithologists' Union, as updated in annual supplements through 2014.

The length and the wingspan in inches for each bird species is included in the accounts. The length measures from the tip of the bill to the end of the tail and the wingspan measures from the tip of the outermost flight feather from one side of the wing across the back to the other wingtip.

There can be considerable variation in the size of individual birds of the same species based on gender, age, or even location. The measurements given in this guide are of average adult birds sourced from Birds of North America Online (BNA Online) bna.birds.cornell.edu and All About Birds (allaboutbirds.org), both websites from the Cornell Lab of Ornithology in Ithaca, New York. These sites are excellent resources for more detailed information about bird life across North America.

Information on distribution, abundance, behavior, and bird vocalizations are given in the main text of each species account. Most accounts have a description of the species vocalizations, often called "voice." Many birds vocalize in complex and varied ways, which can be important for identification. For the purposes of this guide, only the most important vocalizations are described in the species accounts. This also depends on how the bird actually vocalizes in California. For example, many seabirds are not heard while in the state or in the situations most birders encounter them in, so voice descriptions are not provided. More detail is necessary between the Hammond's and Dusky Flycatchers, where voice is one of the most reliable manners of identifying the two.

In cases where the species is broadly distributed in California, general distribution in the state is given. Specific site locations are provided for some species, and when possible, both northern and southern sites in the state.

Specific identification points regarding appearance are in the photo captions along with behavior description when important for identification or simply an interesting thing the bird does.

Getting Started

Now that you have this book, and maybe a pair of binoculars, what do you do? It's easy: Begin where you can look at common birds frequently, and without much travel or investment of time. In other words, where it is easy, such as your backyard. Looking at the backyard species begins to give you some background on the basics, from bird sizes, behaviors, postures, voices, and variations in plumage, just to name a few. From a personal viewpoint, I have been watching and studying birds for decades but still find that backyard birding always brings new questions to mind. I see variations or subtleties I had not noted before, and gain both a great deal of enjoyment and information from doing it. Looking at common birds over and over again is where you gain the skills to expand to less common and seldom seen species. Repetition is important; it is a great mistake to stop looking at a species with care once you have checked it off on your life list. If you keep watching, keep repeating views of all the birds you see, your skills as a birder will only improve.

As you watch in the backyard, or the local parks or nature reserves, you will begin to see fewer and fewer new species. This is expected as you gain more experience with common birds. Of course in time you will want to see some new species. Leafing

Bullock's Oriole is a spectacular backyard bird in California during the spring and summer.

through this book you may be captivated by the Blue Grosbeak, Black-footed Albatross, or Hermit Warbler, species that may be difficult if not impossible to see in the local parks depending on where you live. So plan some outings farther afield to areas in other habitat zones away from where you live. This is always fun and tests your new-found skills as a birder. Use what you know from home to compare to or contrast with your familiar bird, to begin the identification process. As well, make sure that you visit your local areas throughout the year. There are some birds which pass by only in migration (usually spring and fall), others that come to breed (spring and summer), and others that are here in winter only. So a whole set of birds may be missing from your repertoire if you are not birding in the winter, for example. Whatever is your personal method or journey into birding, count yourself as one of the lucky ones. The amazing amounts of fun, joy, mental challenge, sense of accomplishment, and aesthetic beauty you will experience, not only from the birds but the beautiful places birds will take you to makes birding one of the richest and most rewarding of hobbies. There is something for anyone, of any persuasion, of any personality type, and physical abilities in this wonderful hobby.

Bird Identification

The art of identification is like a crossword puzzle, you can become mired up and confused by it, seemingly blocked at times, while at other times it can give you a fantastic sense of accomplishment as you decipher the identify of a bird. Quite simply, bird identification becomes easier as you gain more experience. The key is repetition, seeing things over and over again. With this in mind, looking at common birds is where you really gain experience. They allow you to gain a basis for understanding what birds look like, how they move, feather patterns, songs and any other feature you can think of. When you know the common birds, the less common or unusual will stand out when you see them in your binoculars.

Try to look at birds holistically, in their complete context. So as you watch birds, pay attention to what type of habitat you see them in, and what sounds they make, or any other feature that gets your attention. You can look at birds in a highly detailed level, at the scale of the individual feather. For example, are they pale tipped, marked in their interiors, edged in a different color, or spotted? On the other hand, you can look at the whole bird, seeing major patterns or colors, without looking at the details. Some birders see this as two separate types of birding, two different methodologies of bird identification. I tend to think they are the extremes of the same thing, and as a birder, it is most valuable, and most fun, to see birds in both of these contexts. Sometimes you look and see the whole, and sometimes you concentrate on the details. As you see birds in this multifaceted manner, you will begin to take less and less time to recognize a species. There will come a time when identification will be instant, you will just know that the bird at the feeder is a female House Finch without much thought. At this point you are recognizing rather than identifying, you have gained enough experience that you are short cutting the entire process much like you recognize a friend or family member. The more experience you gain, the more species you will recognize immediately rather than needing to identify through a process of looking at field marks.

Field marks for the very common female House Finch include a long tail, rounded bill, streaky feather pattern below, and a dull face pattern.

What are field marks? These are the specific colors, plumage patterns, bill shapes, or other features that separate a species from another similar species. They are the most important features to look at in making an identification. But thinking about the process described in the previous paragraph, once you have identified a bird to species, don't stop looking at it. Instead, take it all in and then look at its parts. Ask yourself if it has wing bars, the shape of the bill, how long the tail is, if the legs are long or short, what the eye color is, anything you can think of that will make you focus and see elements of the bird that otherwise you might have ignored. A great way to learn is to take field notes, to write things down as you see and document them. The simple act of writing those features down will make you remember them. Even better is to sketch what you see; even a simple sketch (which no one else has to see!) will cement things in your memory. Experiment, have fun with it, and see what works best for you.

Bird Sounds

Learning bird sounds is not as difficult as it may seem. Some of the same basic theory of learning visual bird identification applies to learning the bird sounds, mainly that repetition and experience are key. Musical ability does not particularly help or hinder the ability to learn bird sounds. Besides remembering the "tune" of the bird vocalization, experienced birders seem to process the quality of the sound, the pitch range and overall length of the song in their recognition of the sound. Like visual identification, eventually you know the sound well enough that it becomes almost instant recognition.

You can practice learning bird sounds by using a computer application on a smart phone, an MP3 player, a tablet, or a CD. This is a great way to hear the diversity of bird sounds, but your brain becomes awfully muddled after you have heard three or four different species back to back. Up to three or so you can make sense of the sounds, compare them, and recall them. But as you add more to your learning sessions, it can become terribly confusing. Perhaps the best use of apps and CDs is to

Although drab in appearance, the song of the Brewer's Sparrow is complex and beautiful and easy to identify.

isolate pairs or trios of birds which you think sound similar and you have trouble with (such as American Robin, Black-headed Grosbeak, and Western Tanager) and then compare and contrast these troublesome birds to be better prepared in the field the next time you encounter these sounds.

Observing and noting birds at certain times of the day, seasons, or in particular habitats will reinforce your knowledge of birds. The Lincoln's Sparrow is best seen in the moist, densely vegetated habitats it prefers.

Context: Habitats and Behavior

The importance of context in making bird identifications cannot be understated. When you see a Lincoln's Sparrow in winter, coming out of dense moist shrubbery, all of these things come together in your mind as the *context* for your observation of this bird. As this happens over and over again, you will gain a sense of *déjà vu* and when you are in that same context of time of year and type of habitat, you will almost instinctively search for a Lincoln's Sparrow and low and behold eventually you will find them. The idea of context is not only about habitat, but habitat plus time of year, time of day, weather, and various other factors that influence when and how you see a bird. The more you pay attention to habitat, and context, the more helpful it will be for you in future birding forays.

Habitat is the description of where you find a bird. In most cases habitat refers to the types of plants, or plant associations (ponderosa pine forest, or coastal chaparral) that a bird prefers. Yet, habitat may involve no plants at all such as in mudflats, beaches, and the open ocean. Additionally, some birds are very particular, so ponderosa pine forest may be a prerequisite, but they may require open understory within that forest, or widely spaced and large trees. Habitat descriptions can be a broad brush, or very specific. Some bird species are extremely specific, and others are very general in the habitats they accept. Part of the joy of birding is that you not only learn to identify birds by name, but you learn about their lives and life histories. As you head out birding, you will pick up these details on habitat choices, which species are specialists and which are generalists.

Behavior is anything the bird does, from wagging the tail, how lively its movements are, where it nests, and how it sings, etc. Aspects of a bird's behavior can be very important in identifying and getting to know birds. Some behavior is obvious and some is subtle. The tiny swallows and swifts fly at high speed shifting directions briskly and hardly ever seem to land. This acrobatic aerial behavior is an excellent behavioral clue. More subtle may be the way that a Say's Phoebe wags its tail with a slight flare, while the Black Phoebe wags without flaring. The more you pay attention to what a bird does, the more bits of behavioral

The spectacular Violet-green Swallow spends much of its time in acrobatic flight hunting insects on the wing.

The immature Brown Pelican (left) undergoes a dramatic change in plumage when it reaches adulthood and acquires its breeding colors, as this adult male (right).

information you pick up that will help to identify a species. Again, if you write these observations down in a notebook, you will remember them much more readily the next time you see that Say's Phoebe or other bird with a behavioral clue to its identification.

As you venture farther afield, and gain more experience in birding, you will find that there are variations. Just like people, no two birds are exactly alike. Some of this variation is explained by differences in age or sex, and others are entirely individual. In a large flock of Marbled Godwits, if you look with care you will see that some individuals are bigger and bulkier, and not only that, they also have longer bills and legs. These are the females! Female Marbled Godwits are distinctly larger and have longer extremities than the males; the difference is due to their slightly different ecological niches. Females feed in deeper water than the males.

The young nonbreeding male Western Tanager (top) will become far more colorful as the breeding season approaches in the spring and summer (bottom).

Many species have slightly or radically different plumages as immatures and as adults. Those brown gulls you see in the flocks of pristine white and gray adults are the immatures. Gulls undergo several stages of immature plumage before reaching adult feathering. Keep in mind that some odd looking birds you may see in the field could be the young of a species you know well. Concentrate on sizes, shapes, and behavior to help you identify immature birds—these aspects are more consistent than plumages in many cases within a species. Also keep in mind some general patterns that occur. One is that large birds take more time to fully mature than small birds. Eagles and Brown Pelicans have several different stages of immaturity, while an Anna's Hummingbird or Song Sparrow have only one. Some species fledge with a plumage that is essentially like the adult, so they have only adult plumages throughout their life as in Sooty Shearwater or Wrentit. Second, is that species in which the male is much brighter than the female, often the first-year male has an intermediate plumage, which combines male and female features, as in young male Hooded Orioles.

Another pattern is that many birds that are particularly bright during the breeding season may shift to a dull plumage in the nonbreeding season. Note that the Western Tanager male becomes much less colorful in fall, yet its relative the Summer Tanager remains fully red and bright throughout the year. Learning which birds have different plumage patterns will greatly assist in field identification.

Parts of a Bird

Describing a bird's appearance, often called its "morphology," requires a large vocabulary of specialized scientific terms. Though highly technical terms have been avoided as much as possible in the main text and captions of this guide, some special terms are used. The following illustrations with captions point out the prominent aspects of four major groups of birds: ducks, gulls, raptors, and songbirds.

flank
back
bill
tail
undertail coverts
flank
neck
scapulars

PARTS OF A DUCK
This adult male Northern Pintail shows major parts of a duck's body as it rests on the water.

crown
iris
orbital ring

PARTS OF A GULL
This adult Western Gull in summer plumage shows colors and some body parts visible on a gull or shorebird as it rests on a beach.

gape
throat
breast
belly
tail
primaries (flight feathers)

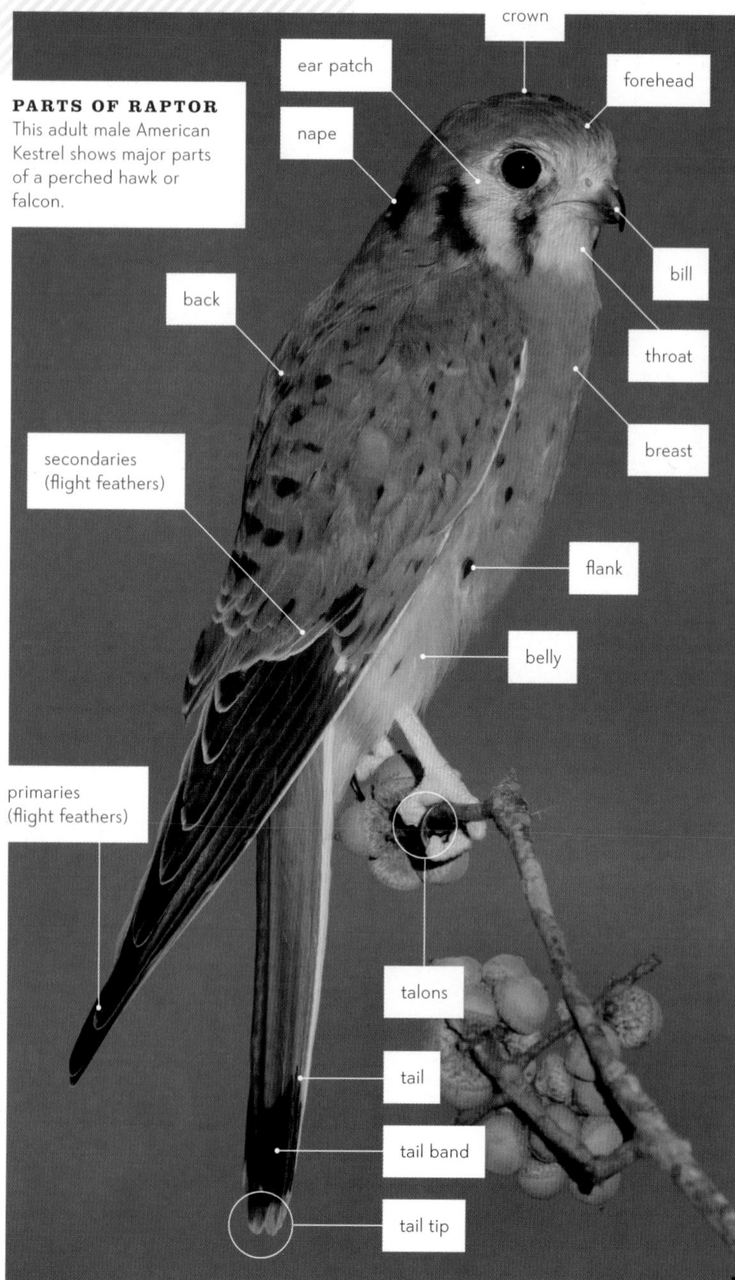

PARTS OF RAPTOR
This adult male American Kestrel shows major parts of a perched hawk or falcon.

PARTS A SONGBIRD
This adult White-crowned Sparrow shows major body parts and field marks of a perched songbird.

Birding California

California is certainly one of, if not *the*, "birdiest" states. So you can imagine that to see a wide selection of the birds of California, you would have to travel great distances, and perhaps also in different seasons! So if you had to choose a list of places to visit that would get you to experience a wide assortment of birds found in the state, where would these be? What are the spots that are great for birds, or absolutely unique? Some of the birding sites in California are of world importance to birds, such as Mono Lake, or Monterey Bay, while others are superb places, but perhaps not of such international birding significance. This is not meant to be a complete list, but it is a start, and rest assured that if you visit all of these places you will encounter not only an amazing assortment of birds, but some of the most gorgeous natural areas in the state.

NORTHWESTERN CALIFORNIA

In the Arcata-Eureka area, there are some fantastic birding sites. Arcata Marsh is the single spot where more species of birds have been found anywhere in the northwest of the state. There are various trails and habitats to explore, and watch for the Redwood Region Audubon Society's Saturday marsh walk. Farther south is the North Jetty of the channel connecting the ocean to the Humboldt Bay. This is an excellent spot to watch migrating loons, Surf Scoter, and perhaps Harlequin Duck. The rock-loving shorebirds, the "rock pipers" can be sought after here: Surfbird, Black Turnstone, and Wandering Tattler. The rare Rock Sandpiper can show up here, as well. In Humboldt Bay, a place to visit is the Salmon Creek Unit of Humboldt Bay NWR. This is a very good spot to see the Aleutian subspecies of the Cackling Goose, as well as varieties and numbers of waterfowl. It is also an area good for herons, American Bittern, rails, and raptors.

Farther north, Prairie Creek State Park is a forested preserve with the classic deep forest birds of the Pacific Northwest, including Varied Thrush, along with the more common species. For the intrepid, a pre-dawn visit in the summer allows one to hear the daily movement of Marbled Murrelets from the ocean to

Surf Scoters may be seen beyond the surf and near jetties and the channel of Humboldt Bay.

their forest nesting grounds. It is one of the few spots in California where you can experience this. Pileated Woodpeckers Northern Pygmy-Owls, and Vaux's Swifts are here, and the coast offers seabird watching as well. In Del Norte County one finds Castle Rock, which is the second largest seabird colony in the state after the Farallon Islands. This is the only spot in California where you can see a Tufted Puffin from shore, particularly in spring in the early part of their breeding season. This is an outstanding area to see loons, scoters, all three cormorants, as well as breeding Common Murres, and Pigeon Guillemots.

NORTHEASTERN CALIFORNIA

This area is a mix of important wetlands, mountains, and conifer forests. The highlights from a birder's perspective are the wetlands of the Lower Klamath National Wildlife Refuge and Tule Lake National Wildlife Refuge. These two sites are part of a complex that includes various locations on the Oregon side of the border, all part of the Klamath Basin region. The wintering waterfowl here can be amazing, particularly in the late winter when northbound migration is beginning. Counts of 30,000 Greater White-fronted, Snow, and Ross's Geese can be experienced at this time of year. Similarly, tens of thousands of Tundra Swans can be seen here, along with thousands of ducks, particularly, of American Wigeon, Mallard, Northern Shoveler, and Northern Pintail. The wintering raptors here are also a draw, where a daily count of over 100 Bald Eagles is common. Raptors that are rare in California overall can be frequent here, such as Rough-legged Hawks.

Wintering Snow Geese find excellent habitat in the national wildlife refuges of northeastern California.

CENTRAL VALLEY

Best known in the Central Valley are the various National Wildlife Refuges, both in the Sacramento and San Joaquin Valleys. These are incredibly important for migratory waterfowl, and in winter can have hundreds of thousands of geese and ducks. The San Luis National Wildlife Refuge Complex, includes the San Luis and Merced NWRs. These are great places

The California endemic Yellow-Billed Magpie (left) and the more wide-ranging Oak Titmouse (right) are both found in the Cosumnes River Preserve, one of the last stands of valley oak in the Central Valley.

to study Snow and Ross's geese, as well as an abundance of ducks. The fields may hold wintering Long-billed Curlews and White-faced Ibis, and watch for Yellow-billed Magpies in the trees. In summer, Tricolored Blackbirds nest in the area. Farther north you will find the Sacramento NWR complex, Colusa NWR, and Greys Lodge NWR to name a few; all of these are wonderful areas to see wintering geese by the thousands, ducks, and hawks and sometimes Bald Eagles. Sandhill Cranes may be found in the winter and migration, and watch the marshes for American Bitterns among the reeds.

Near the town of Thornton, south of Sacramento, there is a special spot, the Cosumnes River Preserve. This preserve managed by the Nature Conservancy is considered the best remaining forest of valley oak in the Central Valley. The preserve also has a varied set of habitats, so it is great any time of year for wintering or breeding birds. It is a great place to see Yellow-billed Magpie as well as other birds associated with oaks, such as Nuttall's Woodpeckers and Oak Titmice. In the breeding season, Blue Grosbeaks are here, and in winter migratory waterfowl, sparrows and raptors can be seen.

CENTRAL COAST

The central coast includes the San Francisco Bay Area, where there are countless of great birding spots. The bay is one of the most important migratory stop over spots for shorebirds on earth! A huge proportion of the entire world population of Western Sandpiper move through here particularly during spring. Thousands of Least Sandpipers, Willets, Marbled Godwits, Dunlin and other species may also be seen. Anywhere mudflats are accessible is a good spot to check, such as the Palo Alto Baylands, Hayward Shoreline, Foster City Shellbar, or the mudflats near Berkeley. The bay is also a major waterfowl wintering area, particularly for Surf Scoter, both species of scaup, and Canvasback. In winter, large numbers of gulls of various species congregate anywhere herring are spawning creating a massive spectacle of avian abundance. This tends to occur in the North Bay, off Richmond or Sausalito.

On the coast itself various areas are a must for the birder. North of the Golden Gate is the Point Reyes National Seashore. In summer, the lighthouse area is a superb place to see the coastal cormorants, Black Oystercatcher, a colony of Common Murres as well as breeding Pigeon Guillemots. In the fall, Point Reyes is known for its lost migratory birds. When the right conditions occur, a variety of eastern migrants, often warblers, are found in the isolated stands of trees on the outer point. Shorebirds migrate through the area, and the Abbott's Lagoon is a

Point Reyes National Seashore is an ideal spot to enjoy the brightly billed Black Oystercatcher.

fantastic place to see them, often unusual species. In fall, immediately north of the Golden Gate is Hawk Hill, certainly the best place to see migrating hawks in coastal California. Official counters tally the numbers as the birds go by from the Golden Gate Raptor Observatory, and often banding is occurring as well and they may bring out hawks to show before the banders are released.

Farther south is the San Mateo County coastside, and the town of Half Moon Bay. Varied habitat types are found here and it is an ideal spot to see migrants, but it is worthwhile to visit at any time of year. In winter the flocks of gulls on the beach, particularly at the mouth of Pilarcitos Creek, or in Pillar Point Harbor are good places to find Thayer's Gull, as well as an abundance of Glaucous-winged Gulls, and sometimes even more unusual species. Also look for wintering Snowy Plovers immediately south of the creek mouth. Recently Half Moon Bay has become a very popular area to embark on a pelagic birding trip. Some trips from here head out offshore to observe

The handsome Hermit Warbler nests in the Sierras, where its high-pitched song may be heard during the late-spring and summer.

seabirds, including Black-footed Albatross, shearwaters, and alcids. In August, several trips to the Farallon Islands are available. The Farallon Islands are the largest seabird breeding colony south of Alaska, and the best spot in California to see the Tufted Puffin. The coastside is good for finding Marbled Murrelet, and in the right time of year, migrating loons, Brant, and Surf Scoter.

Similarly, various boats head out to whale watch or for pelagic birding trips out of Monterey Harbor in Monterey Bay. The bay is the largest and deepest underwater canyon essentially anywhere on earth. This deep water close to shore allows for a concentration of food, often creating a bonanza of birds and whales. The Moss Landing area is great for watching shorebirds and sea otters. The Elkhorn Slough just inland can be a superb spot for birding—large flocks of Tricolored Blackbirds winter here.

SIERRA

The Cascades-Sierras are an important barrier to birds from the moister west side and the more arid east side. Various species found in the mountains do not venture much into the lowlands, such as the Clark's Nutcracker, Cassin's Finch, Williamson's Sapsucker, to name just a few. An outstanding spot in the Sierras not only for the birds, but for the amazing Giant Sequoias, is Calaveras Big Trees State Park. With lots of luck, one may run into the rare Spotted Owl here, but more frequent are the Pileated and White-headed Woodpecker, Red-breasted Sapsucker, Mountain Chickadee, Townsend's Solitaire, breeding Fox Sparrow, Hermit Warbler, and may more mountain birds. Similarly Yosemite National Park offers not only great birding, but world-class scenery. There are many trails and areas to visit. Two noteworthy areas are Crane Flat, where the rare Great Gray Owl is sometimes seen, but more expected are the Hammond's and Dusky Flycatchers, MacGillvray's Warbler, and Lincoln's Sparrow. Farther upslope is Tuolomne Meadows, where Williamson's Sapsucker, Clark's Nutcracker, Mountain Bluebird, breeding White-crowned Sparrow, and Cassin's Finch may be found in summer. One may continue up and over the Sierras to Mono Lake, where sagebrush and drier forest habitats occur for a great birding road trip.

The male Greater Sage-Grouse courts females with a magnificent display in the high desert of the eastern Sierra Nevadas.

EAST OF THE SIERRA

East of the Sierra is part of the Great Basin. This region is known for its high desert and large expanses of sagebrush. This habitat attracts Greater Sage-Grouse, Sage Thrasher, and Sagebrush Sparrow. The sage-grouse is easiest, although not easy, to find at the historic ghost town of Bodie. Mono Lake, a bit farther south, is one of the most important bodies of water for birds in California. In summer, a huge breeding colony of California Gulls breeds here. As their breeding winds down in the late summer, large numbers of southbound Wilson's Phalaropes congregate in this hypersaline body of water. The next species to come down and mass at the lake is the Eared Grebe. For these three species, Mono Lake is a crucial habitat. Other interesting species can be found east of the Sierra in the foothills or pinyon-juniper habitats, including Pinyon Jay, Juniper Titmouse, as well as the "Woodhouse's" subspecies of the Western Scrub-Jay.

SOUTH COAST

This area includes the highly urbanized areas of Los Angeles and San Diego. While urban, it still has many superb areas for birding. A unique trip at the north end of this region is a boat trip to Santa Cruz Islands, in the Channel Islands. Boats leave from Ventura Harbor. Santa Cruz Island is the only place where you can see the endemic (found nowhere else on Earth) Island Scrub-Jay, and on the way you may run into Scripps's Murrelets, all three cormorant species, Brown Pelicans, and perhaps Black-vented Shearwater, depending on the time of year. A visit to the highlands of the San Gabriel Mountains is fantastic, particularly during the breeding season, along the Angeles Crest Highway. You can find American Dipper, Mountain Quail, White-headed Woodpecker, Williamson's Sapsucker, Clark's Nutcracker, Green-tailed Towhee and Black-chinned Sparrow, among the many possibilities. In Huntington Beach, the amazing

The Bolsa Chica Wetlands Ecological Preserve is a major breeding ground for terns, including the boldly crested Royal Tern.

Bolsa Chica Wetlands Ecological Preserve is to be found. This is a great spot for migratory shorebirds, as well as breeding terns and Black Skimmer. You can find Royal and Elegant Terns, as well as Forster's and Least Terns here. In the salt marsh the dark "Belding's" subspecies of the Savannah Sparrow is common.

In the San Diego area, Point Loma is a fine place to look for migratory birds, particularly in September and October, although spring migration is also good. Seabirds often come closer to land here than in other spots in the county, so watching with a spotting scope is advised here in late summer and fall. Otherwise look for one of the many southern California pelagic trips, some of which head out from San Diego to get up close and personal with the southern California seabirds. The Tijuana River estuary can yield Ridgway's Rails on the high tide, and close to the coast, Least, Elegant, and Royal Terns, herons and egrets, as well as migratory land birds. Farther

The Le Conte's Thrasher is a year-round resident of California's southeastern desert.

inland in riparian scrub, watch for Bell's Vireo, Yellow-breasted Chat, Blue Grosbeak, and migrant landbirds. Inland in the county, a great spot to visit is Kitchen Creek Road (about 50 miles east of the city), where Gray Vireo, Mountain Quail, Lawrence's Goldfinch, Black-chinned Sparrow, and Phainopepla may be discovered. Continuing east, the Anza-Borrego Desert State Park is gorgeous and birdy. Watch for Scott's Oriole, Black-tailed Gnatcatcher, Black-throated Sparrow, Cactus Wren, and Costa's Hummingbird.

DESERT

There are three different types of desert in California. East of the Sierra and farthest north is the Great Basin Desert with its sage flats, mentioned in the "East of the Sierra" section above. Farther south is the high desert, or Mojave Desert, and south of that, the lower Sonoran Desert. Death Valley and Joshua Tree National Park are both in the Mojave. Cottonwood Spring is a superb spot to bird in Joshua Tree. Watch for Scott's Oriole, Gambel's Quail, Black-throated Sparrow, Rock Wren, Cactus Wren, and Greater Roadrunner. The Sonoran Desert zone includes the largest lake in the state, the Salton Sea. This is an accidental lake created when the Colorado River was accidentally diverted in 1905. The Salton Sea and the nearby Sonny Bono National Wildlife Refuge hold amazing numbers of wintering waterfowl. The water is hypersaline and will sometimes attract lost seabirds. It is known as the best place in the U.S. to see the Yellow-footed Gull. Agricultural areas nearby teem with White-faced Ibis, migratory geese, Cattle Egret, and sizeable numbers of the Burrowing Owl. In mesquite scrub, watch for Crissal Thrasher, and in dry and more open areas the Le Conte's Thrasher; the Abert's Towhee is common in riparian thickets and parks.

Additional Resources

For nature lovers who wish to learn more about the birds of California, and the rest of North America, two prominent and useful illustrated bird field guides are recommended: *National Geographic Field Guide to the Birds of North America* by Jon Dunn and Jonathan Alderfer (National Geographic, 2011) and *The Sibley Guide to Birds* by David Sibley (Knopf, 2014). An excellent photographic field guide to birds is the *Smithsonian Field Guide to the Birds of North America* by Ted Floyd (Collins, 2008); it also contains a DVD of bird vocalizations.

Two authoritative sources of information online are the Cornell Lab of Ornithology's All About Birds (allaboutbirds.org) and eBird (ebird.org), where users can see current and historical maps of bird observations, record birds sightings, keep track of bird lists, share sightings with the eBird community, and contribute to citizen science.

There are more than 40 local Audubon Society chapters in California; a listing of chapters are found online at ca.audubon.org/audubon-locations.

American Birding Association

Field Guide to Birds of California

Canada Goose

Branta canadensis

L 30–43" | **WS** 50–67"

Hunters know the Canada Goose, the largest goose in California, as the "honker." It's not a bad name for this noisy bird with its loud resonant call. Now widespread, the Canada Goose was once only a migrant and wintering species in California; wild geese still spend the nonbreeding season at Central Valley refuges, but most of the Canada Geese we see in parks and on golf courses are descended from birds introduced from the Midwest.

Long-necked and long-billed, with black bill and legs. Brown body with paler underparts; black neck highlights a white cheek patch.

Cackling Goose

Branta hutchinsii

L 26″ | **WS** 43″

This diminutive goose has a stubby bill that almost makes it look as if were not fully grown. Highly migratory, it breeds on the Arctic tundra and on Alaska's Aleutian Islands. The Aleutian population was at one time imperiled by nonnative foxes introduced by Russian fur traders. With careful management of fox populations, the Cackling Geese in the Aleutians are now flourishing and have been removed from the endangered species list. Aleutian Cackling Geese now winter and stage in great numbers near Crescent City in the spring, where a well-attended goose festival is held in early May. The call is a cackle, much higher pitched than the call of the Canada Goose; flocks sound like they are yelping excitedly, unlike the measured honking of the Canada Goose.

A miniature Canada Goose, but cuter, with short neck and tiny bill. Head blockier, with steeper forehead. Relatively longer-winged and shorter-legged.

Brant

Branta bernicla

L 24″ | **WS** 43″

California's only marine goose, Brant is a connoisseur of marine algae and eelgrass; it is not common anywhere away from the coast. Morro Bay is an excellent place to find this goose in winter. Brant breed in the high Arctic, arriving in California in October and staying until April or May. West Coast birds, sometimes known as "Black Brant," are darker than those from the Atlantic. Brant migrate over the ocean rather than over land, flying less often in a V-formation than in long snaky lines, often just a few feet above the water. Foraging flocks give quiet, muttering sounds as they feed. The flight call is a short, low-pitched, grating honk.

A small, stocky goose with a short black bill. Dark, with back almost as black as the neck; dark cheek, but a white "bandana" around the neck.

Greater White-fronted Goose

Anser albifrons

L 28″ | **WS** 53″

This goose is known colloquially as the "specklebelly" after the adult's variable black barring on its underparts. It's particularly noticeable in flight. Young-of-the-year birds lack the white front and speckled belly, and can be confused with larger-bodied domestic geese. Greater White-fronted Geese are strong migrants, heading to the Arctic tundra and boreal forests to breed. This very social goose is found in the thousands during the nonbreeding season, preferring areas that mix marshes and agricultural fields, such as Sacramento and Salton Sea NWRs. They fly in classic V-formations; noisy flocks sound like yappy dogs as they fly over.

A large brownish goose with a pinkish bill and orange legs. Adults have white around the bill and blackish barring on the belly. Young birds in fall may lack both, but slowly acquire these markings in the winter.

Snow Goose

Chen caerulescens

L 30″ | **WS** 54″

Some of California's Snow Geese breed in Russian Siberia, coming to spend the nonbreeding period on wetlands and refuges in the Central and Imperial Valleys from October to March. Like most geese, they are highly gregarious, occurring in family groups or in huge flocks of hundreds or even thousands. Often they are found side by side with the very similar Ross's Goose. Young Snow Geese differ from adults in their gray-washed plumage, which becomes progressively more mottled as winter progresses. Central Arctic populations have a dark form (a "morph"), known as the "Blue Goose," once considered a separate species but now recognized as a variant of the Snow Goose. A few Blue Geese winter in California.

The larger of the white geese, with a longer bill and shallower forehead than Ross's. Has a black area ("grin patch") on the cutting edge of the bill.

"Blue Goose" is brown-bodied, with grayish blue wings and white head and neck. Orange bill with grin patch.

Ross's Goose

Chen rossii

L 23″ | **WS** 45″

The Ross's Goose is often found with its very similar but larger relative, the Snow Goose. Mixed flocks of white geese are abundant in the Central and Imperial Valleys, but a close view is often required to confirm the subtle identification features. One of the few birds to breed exclusively in Canada (although there are a few records in Alaska), the Ross's Goose nests on the central Arctic tundra, where populations are booming. Like the Snow Goose, the Ross's also has a dark morph, but it is very rare; look for dark Ross's in the big flocks on Sacramento Valley refuges. Calls are higher pitched and more nasal than in the Snow Goose.

A cute little goose, with shorter bill and neck and steeper forehead than Snow Goose. Bill lacks grin patch, but has blue wash to base.

Tundra Swan

Cygnus columbianus

L 52″ | **WS** 66″

The Tundra Swan is California's only widespread native swan. Unlike the introduced Mute Swan, the Tundra Swan is wild and wary, and unlikely to be found in urban areas. This long-distance migrant breeds in the Arctic. The vast majority of our Tundra Swans are found from November to mid-March in the Sacramento Valley, with superb concentrations, particularly on the northbound migration, in the Klamath Basin and on Tule Lake. It is usually found in family groups foraging in large wetlands and agricultural areas or flocks, flying high in a V-formation. It gives a loud, bugle-like calls.

Huge and entirely white, with classic long neck. Large and long bill has a variably sized yellow spot in front of the eye.

Wood Duck

Aix sponsa

L 20″ | **WS** 27″

No other native duck in North America matches the flamboyant plumage of the male Wood Duck. This duck is a widespread but uncommon resident in California, found on creeks and rivers, often where there are acorn-producing oaks nearby. Wood Ducks are more common in the Cosumnes River Preserve in the Central Valley. Unlike most ducks, "woodies" nest in tree cavities and take well to nest boxes, a boon to conservation efforts. The odd rising whistling calls is reminiscent of Pine Siskin.

A large-headed, crested duck with a long tail. Bright red bill and eyes, green head with striking white accents. Upperparts are iridescent, flanks an unusual yellowish buff.

Female has a distinctive facial pattern, with white Cleopatra makeup around the eye. Puffy, square-shaped head; oddly long tailed. Dappled sides.

Mallard

Anas platyrhynchos

L 22″ | **WS** 34″

Known colloquially by hunters as the "greenhead," this familiar duck is common throughout California on city ponds, lakes, and streams, particularly in the lowlands. In winter, migrants from the north join local birds, many of which winter in the Central Valley. Domestic Mallards are often seen on city ponds. Don't be fooled into thinking a domestic duck is a rare species. These birds come in all shapes and sizes: Some are colored like wild Mallards, but are bulkier, with a large pot belly that is obvious when they stand on land. There are many other domestic types, from blackish with white breasts, to buffy overall, to white with a yellow bill. Male Mallards are usually quiet, giving weak whistles during their wintertime displays. Females quack, often in a descending series.

The male's bright yellow bill contrasts strongly with the shiny green head. Clear white neck ring above warm brown breast. Gray body has a black rear end, with an odd curled black feather above the white tail.

Female warm brown with darker streaking and white tail sides. Paler head with darker eye stripe, orange bill with dark "saddle." Blue patch with white line above and below on wing, sometimes hidden.

In flight, both sexes have blue secondary feathers bordered by white. White tail sides visible on males and females.

Gadwall

Anas strepera

L 20″ | **WS** 33″

Gadwalls generally prefer deeper water than other dabbling ducks, but may be found in shallow fresh or saltwater estuaries in small groups. The numbers of this year-round California resident duck are augmented by migrants during the winter. The highest density of breeding Gadwalls in the Americas is north on the Canada prairies and west on the Great Plains. Gadwalls are usually seen together in mated pairs, making it easier to identify the otherwise challenging female by looking at the more obvious male. In flight, the white square on the wings sets this species apart easily, but that patch can be invisible on swimming birds. The female's bill is dark with an orange edge. Vocally very similar to the Mallard, but the female's quacks are higher pitched.

From a distance, the male is largely gray with a black rear end. Black bill and blocky head give it a distinctive profile. White wing patch is sometimes visible on sitting or swimming bird.

Female similar to Mallard, but has blocky head with steep forehead. Bill tends to look black with orange edge. No obvious white on tail sides; white wing patch often visible.

In flight, both sexes have white patch on secondaries.

Northern Pintail

Anas acuta

L 25″ | **WS** 34″

Though some other duck species have long central tail feathers, they reach an extreme on the well-named pintail. Its long slim profile sets it apart from most ducks. The subtly plumaged male has a white stripe on the side of the neck and seen at close range in the right light, a wonderful bronze or purplish gloss highlights the sides of the neck. With its long neck, the pintail is able to feed in slightly deeper water than other dabblers. While some Northern Pintails breed in California, far more travel to the Midwest and Arctic. Northern Pintails are most in the state in winter, with the highest numbers in Central Valley National Wildlife Refuges. Northern Pintails tend to feed on open water in the day, but at night are found in denser grassy habitats or close to shore.

Long bill and neck, the male sporting a fantastic set of pointed tail feathers. Otherwise grayish with browner head, white breast extending up as a stripe on the side of the neck. Bill blue-gray with black saddle.

Female more grayish brown than other similar ducks, and classic long shape with long neck, long bill, and long, flat body. Facial expression bewildered; lack of pattern makes the beady eye stand out. Tail relatively long and pointed.

In flight, both sexes show long neck. Bronzy speculum bordered cinnamon in front, white at rear.

American Wigeon

Anas americana

L 20" | **WS** 33"

Short-billed and squat-bodied, the American Wigeon has a goose-like shape. Also like geese, it shares the habit of grazing on dry land. Though the American Wigeon also feeds by dabbling in the water, it is common to see foraging flocks in short grass at the edge of a wetland, all "mowing the lawn" in unison. This duck is also known as "baldpate," because the male has a white, "balding" forehead. Wigeons breed in the Arctic as well as on the Great Plains. In California they are found mainly during migration and winter, with a few nesting in the extreme northwest. Males give a loud and distinctive double whistle. The very similar Eurasian Wigeon is regular in very small numbers in winter flocks of American Wigeon.

Small bill looks like blue porcelain dipped in black ink. Long, pointed tail, large head. White forehead contrasts with green face stripe; warm pinkish brown body with white spot before black rear end.

Female grayish brown with warmer flanks. Facial expression is serene, with dark patch around eye. Beautiful waxy blue-gray bill with black tip, thin black outline around base.

Northern Shoveler

Anas clypeata

L 18″ | **WS** 30″

The spoon-shaped bill of the Northern Shoveler has sieve-like edges that help the bird sift through water and mud for food. Shovelers often swim in a flock, with their heads extended and bills swishing from side to side as they strain water for food. Sometimes the flocks swim in a circle, creating a vortex that concentrates food in the center of the circle. Northern Shovelers are particularly fond of shallow and muddy wetlands, even where nearly desiccated. While a few Northern Shoveler breed in California, most are migrants and wintering birds from farther north. Any large wetland will have Northern Shovelers in the non-breeding season, with large numbers in the San Francisco Bay area and the Central Valley.

Male long-bodied, with huge shovel-like black beak. Green head; white breast. Rectangular chestnut flank patch outlined in white. Blue forewing patch with white rear edge in flight.

Female's huge shovel-like bill like male's, but largely orange with dark top. Eye looks small. Streaky plumage and white tail. In flight, pale blue forewing patch.

Blue-winged Teal

Anas discors

L 15″ | **WS** 23″

This species shares the same wing pattern with the Northern Shoveler and the Cinnamon Teal, but the three close relatives sort out by overall mass and bill size. To better understand their relationship and identification, I would have named them the greater, medium, and lesser shovelers. The smallest is the Blue-winged Teal, which also has the smallest bill. Females are often confused with the even smaller, only distantly related Green-winged Teal. Although there are winter visitors to the state, Blue-winged Teal are not numerous in California. Look for them with Cinnamon Teals on wetlands in the Central Valley and Bay Area.

The male is like a French breakfast: café au lait flanks and a croissant on the face! The lead-blue head is visible at close range; the white flank spot and dark rear end show up even at a distance. Note blue forewing patch with white rear border.

Female is a small brown duck, with pale area at bill base and relatively bold face pattern. Slightly cooler brown coloration, smaller bill, and bolder face pattern separate her from Cinnamon Teal. Dull blue forewing patch in flight.

Cinnamon Teal

Anas cyanoptera

L 15″ | **WS** 24″

The "medium-sized shoveler," this species is intermediate in size and bill shape between its close relatives the Northern Shoveler and Blue-winged Teal. It is as blue-winged as the Blue-winged Teal, but it has a larger and wider bill, approaching a shoveler's. It is also more likely to sift the water for food than the Blue-winged. Females of the two are difficult to separate, but keeping bill size in mind helps. The only dabbling duck restricted to the west, the Cinnamon Teal is widespread in California at all seasons, with the largest concentrations in the Central Valley during winter.

Male almost entirely cinnamon, with blackish rear end and golden stripe on scapulars. Bill is shovel-like, but not quite as large as that of the Northern Shoveler. Red eyes, blue forewing patch with white rear border in flight.

Female small with warm brown plumage. Larger-billed than Blue-winged Teal, and lacks strong contrasts on face. Muted dark eye stripe, no obvious white area at base of bill. Dull blue forewing patch in flight.

Green-winged Teal

Anas crecca

L 13″ | **WS** 22″

The smallest duck in North America, this teal is named for its greenish blue wing patch. Like the American Wigeon, the Green-winged will often graze in short grass at the edge of wetlands. A common year-round resident in California, with higher numbers in winter, the Green-winged Teal forms large concentrations on Central Valley refuges such as Gray Lodge NWR, where up to 10,000 have been reported at once. Males are vocal in mid-winter, calling a rolling *preep* that recalls a shorebird's voice.

Compact with small dainty bill. Head chestnut with broad green face stripe. Body gray with triangular creamy-white patch on rear end.

A small and compact duck with a thin and dainty bill. Female is brown with relatively well-marked face pattern; key is the narrow pale stripe below the tail.

In flight, small and stocky. Speculum green and black, with cinnamon border in front.

Canvasback

Aythya valisineria

L 21" | **WS** 33"

The Canvasback is a large, sturdy, and powerful diving duck. Canvasbacks appear pudgy in the water, but they are considered one the fastest flying of ducks, clocked at over 70 mph. Part of its scientific name, *valisineria,* refers to one of its favorite foods, the aquatic wild celery. Canvasbacks root in mud for vegetation, and they also take clams in marine bays. Canvasbacks breed in the Prairie Pothole region and to the north, visiting California only in winter. They are often found sleeping in large flocks in deeper ponds, including waste-water treatment facilities. Much of their feeding takes place during the night.

Male almost entirely cinnamon, with blackish rear end and golden stripe on scapulars. Bill is shovel-like, but not quite as large as that of the Northern Shoveler. Red eyes, blue forewing patch with white rear border in flight.

Shape like male, with ski-jump angle to forehead and long black bill. Grayish body with brown breast and head; weak face pattern with pale stripe behind eye.

Ring-necked Duck

Aythya collaris

L 17″ | **WS** 25″

The brown neck ring of this duck is hardly noticeable against its black neck. More obvious is the white ring on the bill: think of it as the "ring-billed" duck and you will always identify it correctly. Unlike other diving ducks, the Ring-necked is closely tied to freshwater and avoids brackish or salt water. The Ring-necked Duck is not always found in large flocks; sometimes just a single pair or two will be on a smaller woodland pond, a habitat other diving ducks tend to avoid. A winter visitor throughout the state.

Peaked head can look "cone-headed." Bill gray with bold white ring and black tip. Body black with white spur between black breast and gray flanks.

Female can also show cone-headed look. Black bill with white ring. Otherwise uniform brown with pale stripe behind eye and white area at base of bill.

Greater Scaup

Aythya marila

L 19″ | **WS** 30″

The two scaups, Greater and Lesser, are sometimes called "bluebills," and at least in males that is a useful feature distinguishing them from some other diving ducks. Identification to species is extremely tricky, as it relies mainly on differences in shape and size rather than markings. The two scaup are commonly found together, though on average the Greater Scaup is found in more marine habitats than the Lesser; some of the highest numbers in the state are found wintering in San Francisco Bay, where they dive for vegetation and clams. The Greater Scaup is a far northern breeder, raising its young on ponds in the boreal forest.

Male blue-billed and pale-bodied with black breast. Similar to Lesser Scaup, but head rounded, bill larger, and glosssy green plumage, though it changes with light.

Female uniform brown with grayer back and large white patch at base of dark bill. Similar to Lesser Scaup, but head rounded rather than peaked, bill larger.

Lesser Scaup

Aythya affinis

L 17″ | **WS** 29″

This is the smaller of the "bluebills," much more closely tied to freshwater habitats, although the two species of scaup are often found together. The Lesser Scaup breeds much farther south than the Greater, and some breed in northern California. A common winter visitor, this is the expected scaup inland, with the highest concentrations in the Central Valley. Identification relies mainly on shape and size differences, but the Lesser Scaup has a noticeably more restricted white wing stripe in flight. While there is an average difference in the color of the iridescence on the head, the apparent color changes with the lighting, making this a character to be used with reservation.

Male blue-billed and pale-bodied with black breast. Similar to Greater Scaup, but shows peaked crown, smaller bill with restricted black tip, tendency to purple in the iridescent head, and slightly darker body.

Female brown with grayer back and white patch at base of bill. Like Greater, but has a peaked head, smaller bill.

Surf Scoter

Melanitta perspicillata

L 23″ | **WS** 30″

Known colloquially as the "skunkhead," the adult male Surf Scoter has a striking black and white head pattern. By far the most common of California's three scoter species, Surf Scoters are chiefly a winter resident in California, however, a few immature birds summer over in small numbers. The Surf Scoter is found on nearshore waters and large brackish bays; an estimated 80,000, the largest concentration in the state, winter on San Francisco Bay. Surf Scoters dive to feed mainly on mollusks.

Large ocean-going duck with black body that sets off white eye and head patches. Bill ridiculously colored, with rounded dark patch at its base.

Female with a distinctly square, flat-topped head. Two white patches on head, one in front and one behind eye, contrasting with dark cap.

White-winged Scoter

Melanitta fusca

L 21″ | **WS** 31″

This scoter is much less common than the Surf Scoter, with which it usually flocks. Larger and longer, it is always separated from the other scoters by the white wing patch. White-wings breed in the western boreal forest and migrate to coastal areas for the winter. The bulk of the western population winters north of California, although one can find White-winged Scoters anywhere along the coast or in San Francisco Bay in winter. They dive for mollusks and feed largely during the day. Like other scoters, White-wings fly in long loose lines, making the white on the wings obvious.

Large ocean-going duck; male with black plumage and white wing patch, often visible when swimming. Distinctive white "Nike swoosh" below eye, and orange pink bill with blackish knob at base.

Female with oval white patch on side of head and base of bill.

Black Scoter

Melanitta americana

L 19" | **WS** 33"

This is the least common and the smallest of our three scoters. Like the White-winged, the Black Scoter is usually found in flocks of the more common Surf Scoter. Male Black Scoters are colloquially known as "butterbills" because of the bright yellow blob on the black bill. Like other scoters, they are winter visitors to California, where they can show up anywhere along the coast; the bulk of the population winters in British Columbia. This scoter breeds on more northern tundra than the other two. It dives for mollusks, usually in water less than 30 feet in depth.

The all-black male has a butter-colored area on the base of the black bill.

Smallest of the scoters, with relatively standard-shaped duck bill. Female entirely brown with contrasting pale cheek and dark cap. Often swims with tail cocked up.

Ruddy Duck

Oxyura jamaicensis

L 15″ | **WS** 23″

The Ruddy Duck is a "stiff-tailed" duck—a bulky-bodied diving duck with a typically upturned tail. Unlike most ducks, which are in their brightest plumage in winter, the Ruddy loses its glow during the cooler months. Ruddy Ducks are often seen sleeping in groups, often in the middle of a pond; they commonly feed at night. One almost never sees Ruddy Ducks in flight, as they are nocturnal migrants. Both breeding and wintering in California, males perform a head-bobbing display and make popping, frog-like sounds.

Male is a small stocky duck with bull-neck and spiky tail. Breeding plumage chestnut with white cheek and baby-blue bill. In winter, brown with dull bill, but retains white cheek.

Female shaped like make, small and stocky with spiky tail. Uniform brown, with dark cap and dark stripe on pale cheek.

Common Goldeneye

Bucephala clangula

L 18″ | **WS** 32″

The goldeneyes and mergansers are closely related, and almost all breed in tree cavities. Common Goldeneyes breed on forest ponds mainly in Canada, and come to California during the non-breeding season. They are found from October to April in both freshwater and marine habitats, preferring sheltered areas. The highest numbers are found on deeper ponds and reservoirs in the Central Valley. They dive for their food, which includes invertebrates and plants. When displaying, males throw their head back while giving an odd frog-like noise that is reminiscent of the call of a Common Nighthawk.

A conspicuous diving duck with a largely white body and black rear end and back. The large head has a rounded triangular shape; it often shows green gloss. Bright yellow eye, circular white patch at base of black bill.

Female is a compact diving duck with bright yellow eye on puffy brown head. Body cold gray, white neck ring below brown head; white patches on wing often visible on swimming bird. The bill is black, usually with a yellow tip.

Barrow's Goldeneye

Bucephala islandica

L 18″ | **WS** 30″

The less common of the goldeneyes, the Barrow's is almost always found in flocks of Common Goldeneyes. Its odd breeding distribution includes the Rocky Mountains and Labrador. Western Barrow's winter most commonly at the latitude of British Columbia, less frequently southward. The winter range in California is very precise; one of the most accessible and reliable spots is Lake Merritt in downtown Oakland. Goldeneyes are divers, feeding on animal and vegetable prey. Hunters call both species whistlers because of the loud wing noise; the Barrow's appears to be slightly quieter in flight than the Common.

Male similar to Common Goldeneye, but steeper forehead, tendency to blue or purplish gloss on head, and white crescent on face. Body more blackish, with pattern of white "portholes" on side; black spur at breast side reaches to water.

Female similar to Common Goldeneye, but smaller bill usually entirely orange-yellow. Steeper forehead, with rounded peak on head tending to be farther forward, and puffy area on nape more noticeable.

Bufflehead

Bucephala albeola

L 14" | **WS** 21"

The Bufflehead is named for its outsized "buffalo head." It is very closely related to the goldeneyes, but has dark eyes and is much smaller, only slightly heavier than a Green-winged Teal. Buffleheads breed on ponds, mostly in Canada, but come south in fall to winter in California. Look for them on freshwater ponds and lakes throughout the state; large numbers congregate in late winter in the Klamath Valley. They often avoid deep water, and are found on smaller, shallower ponds than those preferred by goldeneyes and scaup.

Male is a small, cute duck with a short dark bill. Large puffy head iridescent blackish with large white patch. White from breast to tail base, black on back.

Female is a small, large-headed duck with a small dark bill. Body is gray and head browner, with a noticeable white oval on the cheeks.

Hooded Merganser

Lophodytes cucullatus

L 17" | **WS** 25"

The mergansers are fish-eating ducks, though the Hooded Merganser also takes invertebrate prey. Hoodies are fond of wooded ponds and rivers. The western population breeds mainly in British Columbia, wintering in small numbers south to California, mainly west of the Sierras. Hooded Mergansers are most common in the north, with good numbers wintering along rivers in the Central Valley, in the Klamath Region, and on Lake Almanor.

Long, narrow bill, large head with white wedge. Crest can be lowered, making head look flat-topped. White breast with two black spurs that reach to water, gorgeous cinnamon flanks. Long tail sometimes cocked.

Long, narrow bill, with large head and long tail that is sometimes cocked. The female is brown, with a paler breast and warmer cinnamon head. The head can look flat-topped when crest down, large and puffy when raised.

Common Merganser

Mergus merganser

L 24″ | **WS** 33″

This merganser is particularly fond of rivers in California. Common Mergansers breed in large tree cavities or broken stumps along forested waterways. During the non-breeding period, they can be found in more open habitats, such as reservoirs and lakes. After strong rains, increased river flow may drive them to nearby lakes or ponds. Large concentrations are found in winter on Lake Isabella. This merganser is largely a fish-eater, but is also fond of frogs and other aquatic animals taken by diving.

Large and long-bodied, mainly white with black back and green head. Long bill bright red.

Large, long body mainly gray with paler breast. Shaggy crest on cinnamon head. Distinguished from Red-breasted by bold white throat patch and distinct line separating pale breast from cinnamon neck.

Red-breasted Merganser

Mergus serrator

L 22″ | **WS** 27″

The Red-breasted Merganser is the only member of the goldeneye and merganser group that does not breed in a tree cavity. Instead, this species builds its nest on the ground, allowing it to breed north of the tree line in the Arctic and subarctic regions. Highly migratory, Red-breasted Mergansers visit California during the non-breeding season, when they are strictly marine, diving for fish and other animal prey. The Red-breasted Merganser is North America's fastest duck, clocked at 100 mph.

Green head with punky spiked haircut; bold white neck band above reddish brown breast. Body gray, white, and black, with odd white-centered feathers on breast side.

Long merganser bill and shaggy crest. Similar to female Common, but crest shaggier, head duller brown; poorly defined pale throat and messy transition between brown neck and paler breast.

California Quail

Callipepla californica

L 10″ | **WS** 14″

This gorgeous terrestrial species is the state bird of California. Particularly in spring and early summer, males are obvious as they proclaim their territory with a nasal three-syllable call sometimes paraphrased as *chi-ca-go!* Later in the season, the females and young are commonly seen; young birds can fly when less than half-grown. Although highly adaptable, the California Quail has been doing very poorly in the city of San Francisco, where predation by housecats has driven the species nearly to extinction. Except in the desert southeast, look for this quail throughout the state in any area with chaparral, or on shrubby forest edge.

Male is a truly "wow" bird: gorgeous plumage with black topknot, rusty belly bordered by scaly pattern.

Female a toned-down version of the male, with small topknot. Gray body, white-streaked flanks.

Gambel's Quail

Callipepla gambelii

L 9" | **WS** 13.5"

The Gambel's Quail is resident in arid desert habitats of the southeast. Concentrations can be found in the Mojave National Preserve and other desert habitats with taller or shrubby vegetation; Gambel's Quail do particularly well near towns or villages. The voice is similar to that of the California Quail. This quail is fond of seed feeders in desert towns and parks.

Male with black topknot and rusty crown, black belly bordered in creamy buff, chestnut flanks with pale streaks.

Female gray overall with pale streaked chestnut flanks and white underparts.

Mountain Quail

Oreortyx pictus

L 11″ | **WS** 14.5″

The well-named Mountain Quail is easiest to find in the spring, when males are vocalizing with a loud two-syllable *We-Aark!*, repeated after a pause. This shy species can be difficult to find the rest of the year, though it is widely distributed in mountainous areas; a particularly good area is the Pacific Crest Trail off Kitchen Creek Road in San Diego, where the open vegetation makes it easier to see. Farther north in the San Gabriel Mountains, the trail to Monrovia Peak can also be good.

Straight black topknot unique among our quail. Flanks rusty with broad parallel white bars; chestnut throat with white stripe below eye. Female similar but duller.

Ring-necked Pheasant

Phasianus colchicus

L 24" | **WS** 28"

Introduced to North America for sport, many populations of the Ring-necked Pheasant, including some in California, are still stocked annually for hunting. Male pheasants can be conspicuous, but females are more difficult to find. The highest populations in the state are in the Central Valley, with some found as far south as the Imperial Valley. Pheasants are found in agricultural and grassland habitats and in scrubby edge with openings. A population persists in the south part of San Francisco Bay; Palo Alto Baylands is a good spot to see them. Males give a loud, harsh double honk, followed by noisy whirring wings.

Ornate male with long barred tail. White neck band, red wattles on green head. Colorful body.

Female brownish with long pointed tail.

Greater Sage-Grouse

Centrocercus urophasianus

L 25″ | **WS** 35″

North America's largest grouse, the Greater Sage-Grouse is a resident of sage flats east of the Sierra, where this well-camouflaged species can be difficult to spot, especially when the birds stay very still. A great place to find them is the ghost town of Bodie, north of Mono Lake. Early in the spring, very early in the morning, males display spectacularly on a lek, flaring the tail so that it resembles the top of a pineapple and exposing the white feathers around the neck; two yellow air sacs are inflated to make an odd double-popping sound.

Displaying male amazing: white neck with droopy yellow air sacs, spiky tail.

Large gray-bodied grouse with thick bill and long pointed tail. Adult female with obscure white striping on face, obvious black belly patch.

Sooty Grouse

Dendragapus fuliginosus

L 17.5″ | **WS** 24″

Sooty Grouse are birds of tall conifer forests, where they feed on evergreen needles. They are shy and move very slowly, making them very difficult to find; in the early breeding season, though, males may perch more conspicuously as they give their low hooting song. Displaying males hold their tail up like a fan, raise yellow combs above the eyes, and display yellow air sacs on the breast sides. Sooty Grouse are found in California's northern forests, the coastal mountains south to Mendocino, and the Sierra. Sequoia National Park is a good area to look, as are the forests west and south of Lake Tahoe.

Male large and sooty gray, with pale tip to tail. In display, inflates yellow air sacs on side of neck, flares tail.

Female large and brown, with speckled neck and white triangles on flanks.

Wild Turkey

Meleagris gallopavo

L 42" | **WS** 53"

The Wild Turkey is one of the most unusual birds of our continent, and one of the few bird species in the world to be domesticated for food. Turkeys were introduced in California for hunting. Ironically, those introduced birds are often quite tame, although they become more furtive when hunting season begins. Males in display fan the tail, droop the wings, and raise their body feathers; the facial wattle becomes enlarged and droops over the bill. The distinctive gobble is identical to that of the barnyard version. Turkeys are common throughout most of the state, particularly in oak habitats, but absent from the Central Valley.

Displaying male, or "Tom," distinctive, with pale-tipped tail and blue head with red-wattled neck.

A large and leggy game bird, with naked pink and blue head. Long tail with pale tip, bronzy iridescent body.

Female smaller with less colorful head; both sexes may roost high in trees.

Red-throated Loon

Gavia stellata

L 24″ | **WS** 43″

This is the smallest of the loons, and the only one with a solid brown back in breeding plumage. It gives its identity away in most plumages by holding the bill and head up at an angle, unlike other loons. This Arctic breeder migrates earlier in fall and earlier in spring than other loons, arriving in California as early as September; a few non-breeding immatures may remain all summer, usually retaining their dull nonbreeding plumage. Red-throated Loons can be found at any coastal site in the state. They dive for fish and marine invertebrates. Usually silent in California.

Breeding plumage has gray head and deep red throat, brown body with indistinct white spots.

Holds head and thin bill up at an angle. Nonbreeding birds paler on face than other loons.

Pacific Loon

Gavia pacifica

L 26″ | **WS** 47″

The well-named Pacific Loon winters almost exclusively on the Pacific Ocean. Pacific Loons breed throughout the far north in the boreal zone and the subarctic. During migration, particularly in the spring, never-ending streams of Pacific Loons pass Point Reyes, Pigeon Point, Point Pinos, and Point Concepcion. This is the most numerous loon in the state; a few non-breeding immature birds remain through the summer. They are more often found in flocks than the other loons. Silent in California.

Breeding plumage gorgeous, puffy head black at face fading beautifully to pale gray on nape. Checkerboard-patterned back, black and white striped neck and dark throat.

Winter birds brown, with white underparts. Bill held parallel to water's surface. Line dividing dark back of neck from white front of neck straight and smooth; dark "chinstrap."

Common Loon

Gavia immer

L 31″ | **WS** 46″

This is the largest of California's regularly occurring loons, a massive bird when seen close up. The oversized feet, larger than in other loons, show up well in flight. In spite of its name, this is the least common of the three loons in California. Common Loons breed on forested lakes and ponds, mainly in Canada. When migrating with other loons, they often fly higher above the water than other species. This is the only loon that tends to fly over land, and the most likely to be found inland. Common Loons are silent while in California, but are amazing yodelers during the breeding season.

Very big. Breeding bird impressively checkered black and white above, dark head with large black bill, striped neck with full blackish neck band.

Large loon with hefty bill. Nonbreeding bird has dark half collar that extends to mid-neck from neck sides, disrupting division of dark and white.

Pied-billed Grebe

Podilymbus podiceps

L 13.5" | **WS** 21"

This stubby-billed grebe is common throughout California on ponds, lakes, reservoirs, and other wetlands. Like other grebes, they fly only at night. At times they stretch and hold the strongly curved wings up stiffly over the body. They are very good at controlling their buoyancy, sometimes swimming with just the head poking above the water. When frightened, they sink out of sight and disappear for a long time, only poking the bill above water to breathe. The voice is an unusual decelerating series of barking yelps.

A small but stocky grebe with an oversized head and large, thick, almost finch-like bill. In breeding plumage, dark throat and black stripe on bill.

In winter plumage, white throat and plain bill. Fluffy white rear end.

Horned Grebe

Podiceps auritus

L 13″ | **WS** 23.5″

In most places in California, the Horned Grebe is outnumbered by its slightly smaller relative, the Eared Grebe. Horned Grebes breed to the north and east of the state, but winter here. They are most common at coastal sites, but also occur locally on inland lakes and reservoirs; they can be common on Lake Almanor. Horned Grebes are in non-breeding plumage for most of their time in California, but by April some are bright. They dive for invertebrate prey. Silent in California.

Small grebe with pointed and pale-tipped bill and generally flat-topped head. Breeding bird has bold golden stripe above and behind eye, chestnut neck.

Small grebe, bill often pale-tipped, head flat-topped. Slightly larger and thicker-necked than Eared Grebe, with bold white cheek patch and contrasting dark crown.

Eared Grebe

Podiceps nigricollis

L 12″ | **WS** 21″

The Eared Grebe breeds in California away from the coast, and migrants arrive from farther east to spend the nonbreeding season. Eared Grebes are among the few birds that can handle such hyper-saline environments as Mono Lake and the salt ponds in the San Francisco Bay area; in fact, Mono Lake is one of the world's most important sites for this grebe, with an estimated 1.6 million stopping there on migration. Feeding mainly on brine shrimp, the grebes may double their weight, and they also molt their wing feathers to become entirely flightless for a while.

Small, slim-necked grebe. Peaked head with golden ear patch and all black neck in breeding plumage.

Nonbreeders in fall and winter sooty black and white overall. Cheeks dark, white on throat and sides of neck.

Western Grebe

Aechmophorus occidentalis

L 25.5" | **WS** 48"

The Western Grebe and the very similar, closely related Clark's Grebe, were once considered a single species; the two are often found together. Many Western Grebes breed in California, their numbers increased in winter by migrants from the north and east. The courtship display is a marvelous aquatic synchronized dance, culminating when the pair walks on the water. The call of the Western is a two-syllable creaking *kree kree*.

Large grebe with long pointed bill and swan-like neck. Bill dull yellowish to greenish yellow; dark on face reaches below eye, flanks relatively dark.

Clark's Grebe

Aechmophorus clarkii

L 25.5" | **WS** 32"

The Clark's Grebe is often found with the Western Grebe. In winter, some Clark's Grebes have a darker face more like that of the Western, but the brighter bill color still distinguishes them. Both species have a synchronized dance display during the breeding season. Clark's is resident in California, but numbers increase during migration and in winter. The habitats used by the two species sometimes differ: In the Bay area, for example, the Western is the more common species on the coast, while in the South Bay Clark's Grebe is often more common. The Palo Alto Baylands is a good place to see Clark's Grebes. The one-syllable call is a *kreeaa*, higher-pitched than that of the Western Grebe.

Large grebe with long pointed bill and swan-like neck. Bill bright orange-yellow, white around eyes, flanks relatively pale.

Black-footed Albatross

Phoebastria nigripes

L 43″ | **WS** 80″

The large Black-footed Albatross spends most of its life soaring above the waves of the Pacific Ocean. With its seven-foot wingspan, it catches the wind and dips down to the surface to grab squid from the surface of the water. It takes six or seven years to reach maturity and these years are all spent aloft at sea without ever setting foot on land. This albatross breeds on several small islands or atolls in the northwest Hawaiian Islands, but they commonly wander to California at any time of year. The ports of Half Moon Bay, Monterey, and Bodega Bay offer pelagic trips to find this singular bird.

Our most common albatross, with huge narrow wings. All dark with white around bill and under eye. Adults (older than six or seven years) white on uppertail feathers.

Sooty Shearwater

Puffinus griseus

L 17″ | **WS** 41″

The Sooty Shearwater is an abundant seabird that crisscrosses the oceans in search of areas of upwelling with high concentrations of food. They breed in New Zealand, Chile, and Argentina, and migrants arrive in California in March. Numbers build through the summer, peaking in late summer and early fall before the birds return south by November. They can be seen from shore at several sites, including Point Pinos and Half Moon Bay. Near-shore flocks can reach thousands of individuals.

Mid-sized shearwater with narrow wings that look small for the bird, quick mechanical flaps. All dark with narrow bill, white flash on underwing towards wing tip.

Pink-footed Shearwater

Puffinus creatopus

L 18″ | **WS** 43″

The Pink-footed Shearwater is often the most common shearwater seen on a pelagic birding trip. Found farther out on the ocean on average than Sooty Shearwaters, Pink-footeds breed in two island groups in Chile and spend the nonbreeding season in California. Unlike other shearwaters that roam throughout the Pacific, the Pink-footed migrates north and south only through the waters off the Americas. They arrive in California as early as March, and most are heading south by early November. When foraging, excited birds give an exclamatory nasal *nhee!*

A stocky, broad-winged shearwater with short broad tail, mottled white underwing, white belly, and orange-based bill. Slower, lazier flight than Sooty Shearwater.

Black-vented Shearwater

Puffinus opisthomelas

L 14″ | **WS** 32″

The Black-vented Shearwater is the only shearwater that breeds close to California, nesting on three island groups off Baja California. In the nonbreeding season, Black-venteds disperse north. A great place to find them is Point Loma in San Diego; in years of particularly warm water, they may range north to Monterey Bay or even farther, typically peaking in September and October. This species dives for food, mainly anchovies, sardines, or squid, and tends to feed near shore.

Small shearwater with short, slightly rounded wings. Pale below, dark vent, mottled face, and black bill.

Ashy Storm-Petrel

Oceanodroma homochroa

L 7″ | **WS** 16″

The storm-petrels are very small seabirds, some resemble a swallow in flight. The Ashy Storm-Petrel is nearly restricted to California as a breeding species. Half of the world population breeds on the Farallon Islands off San Francisco, most of the rest in California's Channel Islands. This species is not seen from shore, so the best way to find them is to take a pelagic birding boat out of Half Moon Bay, Monterey or Bodega Bay. This species picks food from the surface, and sometimes rests in flocks of hundreds or even thousands.

Small seabird, all dark with forked tail. Pale bar on upperwing, and grayer rump.

Double-crested Cormorant

Phalacrocorax auritus

L 31.5″ | **WS** 46.5″

Common resident throughout California. The Double-crested Cormorant is the only one of our cormorants that is likely to be found inland in freshwater. It is also the only one that regularly flies over land, even along the coast. The Double-crested often flies higher than other cormorants. The distinctive crook in the neck distinguishes it from the marine cormorants. The Double-crested develops short crests in the breeding season, showy white in some individuals and black and hard to see in others. This cormorant often perches with the wings spread, drying them before returning to the water.

Adult is a large, stocky, all-black cormorant with orange skin in front of eye and on throat. Some breeding birds show white crests.

Shows a kink in the neck in flight. Immatures are brownish, paler on the breast and neck.

Brandt's Cormorant

Phalacrocorax penicillatus

L 29″ | **WS** 42.5″

The Brandt's Cormorant is found only on the coast and, to some extent, in San Francisco Bay. This species often forms flocks, and is particularly tied to the small forage fishes, such as, anchovies and sardines, that occur in dense schools. When you see feeding frenzies of Brown Pelicans, gulls, and Common Murres, most of the attending cormorants are Brandt's. A great place to see them is the jetty in Monterey Harbor, where they breed; they are also found in numbers at the lighthouse on Point Reyes and in La Jolla. Brandt's Cormorant flocks tend to fly in loose lines close to the water, sometime with another cormorant species mixed in.

Large and stocky like Double-crested, but has buffy feathered patch at base of mandible. In close view, shows blue bill pouch. Breeding birds have variable pencil-thin white feathers on head and neck. Immature is brown.

Pelagic Cormorant

Phalacrocorax pelagicus

L 25″ | **WS** 42″

This is one of the most poorly named of California birds. "Pelagic" implies that its habitat is offshore, but this is the least likely of our cormorants to be found in the pelagic zone. Pelagic Cormorants do not seem to form single species flocks like the Brandt's, instead foraging singly or joining flocks of Brandt's. The bold white flank patch is present only early in the breeding season. More common on the north coast than southward, Pelagic Cormorants place their nests on cliffs. The lighthouse at Point Reyes is a great place to see this bird.

A small, slim cormorant with tiny head, skinny neck, and long tail. Iridescent head and neck, dull red on face; breeding bird with white flank patch.

Brown Pelican

Pelecanus occidentalis

L 47″ | **WS** 78″

A familiar presence all along the coast and in San Francisco Bay, Brown Pelicans breed mainly on the Channel Islands and in Mexico. After breeding, they disperse to the north; after the first arrivals in May, numbers build into July, before the birds return south by November. Timing numbers vary from year to year with the supply of small forage fish such as anchovies and sardines. When food is scarce, pelicans may not breed at all, and sometimes colonies suffer mass starvation. Like most large birds, Brown Pelicans take several years to mature. Flocks contain a mix of younger, browner birds along with older, grayer birds, with all stages in between. Typically silent.

Adult a huge grayish coastal bird with classic big beak and pouch. Breeding birds with red pouch, brown and creamy yellow head. Winter birds pale-headed.

Immature brown with paler belly. Become progressively more grayish as they age, over several years.

American White Pelican

Pelecanus erythrorhynchos

L 57.5" | **WS** 105"

The bright white plumage of the larger of our two pelican species helps in making it appear downright huge. Weighing in at 16 pounds, white pelicans are one of our heaviest birds. This species is usually found on freshwater, though concentrations of fish can draw them to shallow brackish or even super-saline waters such as Bodega Bay, the San Francisco Bay, and especially the Salton Sea. Breeding American White Pelicans are found in northwest California; migrants and winter visitors occur throughout. Typically silent.

Unique, huge white bird with large orange bill and pouch. Orange legs. Breeding birds have crest and "sail" on bill. Black flight feathers often concealed at rest. Immature washed brown above.

White-faced Ibis

Plegadis chihi

L 20″ | **WS** 36″

In the right light and at the right distance, White-faced Ibis can appear to be the most gorgeous and colorful bird in the world; in duller light or seen from afar, it may appear dull brown or blackish. The White-faced Ibis is a year-round resident in California, mostly away from the coast; migrants from elsewhere also pass through, and even local populations may move with the seasons. Ibis forage on muddy edges or in shallow water; particularly in winter, they can be found on muddy fields and farmland. White-faced Ibis are colonial breeders, and flock at any season. They are especially common in the Central and Imperial Valleys. The quiet calls are nasal grunts.

Chestnut-bodied wading bird with long curved bill and glossy wings. Breeding birds have red face with white border, reddish legs.

In winter, neatly streaked head and neck, pink face, and reddish eye.

In winter, neatly streaked head and neck, pink face, and reddish eye. Probes in shallow water and mud for invertebrates and other food with its long, sensitive, decurved bill.

American Bittern

Botaurus lentiginosus

L 28.5″ | **WS** 36″

A year-round resident in California, the American Bittern is best known as the bird that pretends to be a reed in marsh vegetation. Its remarkable camouflage goes beyond the brown color and striped neck to include behavior: perched birds often point the bill upwards, parallel with the cattail stalks around them. Bitterns flush only reluctantly; in flight, they are big and bulky, with strikingly dark flight feathers. If you visit a marsh where this bird breeds, you may hear one of the oddest sounds made by any North American bird, a booming, gulping *guump galloomp*.

Streaky neck; body with gorgeous marbling.

Least Bittern

Ixobrychus exilis

L 12″ | **WS** 16″

The smallest of our herons, the Least Bittern hides in the marshes like the much larger American Bittern. This is the only California heron in which the male and female have obviously different plumages. Uncommon and generally difficult to see, the Least Bittern is a resident in the south, with small numbers venturing north to the San Joaquin Valley. The wetland reserves around the Salton Sea are great places to look for Least Bitterns. On the breeding grounds, Least Bitterns sing in the evenings and mornings, a cooing *coo–coo–coo*, each note slightly lower-pitched than the one before.

A very small heron, tiny and largely buffy yellowish. Male with black back, female brown-backed.

Great Blue Heron

Ardea herodias

L 38–54″ | **WS** 66–79″

A very large heron, I think of this bird as "old cranky": Great Blue Herons' facial expression appears angry, and when they fly, they give a loud, angry sounding *graaaak!* This is an extremely adaptable bird, foraging for fish and frogs in wetlands and hunting voles and gophers on farm fields. Great Blues breed in colonies, often mixed with Great Egrets, but unlike egrets, they feed singly. Skillful fishermen, they have been seen swallowing prey seemingly big enough to choke them.

Huge blue-gray heron with long neck and legs. Adult has black and white crown, pencil-thin black crest feathers, shaggy plumes on neck and back. Young birds duller, with blackish gray crown.

Great Egret

Ardea alba

L 40″ | **WS** 54″

More closely related to the Great Blue Heron than to other egrets, the Great Egret is a common resident throughout California, breeding in colonies and foraging in wetlands and ditches or on muddy farm fields and grassy vole-rich meadows. The National Audubon Society was founded to stop the "harvest" of egret plumes for use on hats and dresses; this species is now the society's symbol.

Large and white, with bright yellow bill and black legs. Corner of mouth extends to just behind eye.

In flight, typical heron posture with neck folded back. White with yellow beak, legs and toes black.

Snowy Egret

Egretta thula

L 24″ | **WS** 39″

Snowy Egrets are common year-round residents in California, less frequently seen in the north. Snowy Egrets breed in colonies, and feed singly or in loose aggregations in any wet habitat where they can find fish, frogs, or large invertebrates; they are much more likely to be seen in flocks than the Great Egret. The Snowy is intermediate in size between the Great and Cattle Egrets, and slimmer and more elegant. Typically silent.

Smaller than Great Egret. Yellow face, black bill, and black legs with yellow "slippers."

In flight, white with neck tucked in, black legs with yellow feet.

Cattle Egret

Bubulcus ibis

L 20″ | **WS** 36″

This is the smallest and stockiest of the widespread egret species. It is also different ecologically, typically avoiding wetlands in favor of agricultural areas with livestock. Cattle Egrets are common in the Central Valley and in southern California, particularly the Salton Sea and Imperial Valley; they are resident in the south, but most Central Valley birds leave for the winter. This species provides a striking example of natural colonization: in the late nineteenth century, flocks of Cattle Egrets made their way across the ocean from Africa and began breeding in South America; by the 1940s, they had spread to North America, reaching California in 1962.

Stocky, with short, sturdy yellow bill and yellow legs. Breeding bird shows buffy crown, breast, and lower back.

Immature and some non-breeding adults have dark legs.

Green Heron

Butorides virescens

L 17" | **WS** 26"

This dark, crow-sized heron is an uncommon resident in California, more often found on rivers, ponds, and ditches than in extensive marshlands. Green Herons hunt from a shady spot, waiting motionless on a perch or rock before striking at their prey. The tail is frequently flicked downwards, perhaps to attract prey or to draw the prey's attention away from the predator's head and bill. Startled birds often give a loud *kweow* as they fly off. This heron takes well to suburban areas with ponds or canals; a great place to find them in the Bay Area is Foster City.

Small heron with orange legs; rusty, with green tone to wings. Has black bill and black cap. Young birds browner, more streaked.

Black-crowned Night-Heron

Nycticorax nycticorax

L 24" | **WS** 45.5"

The scientific name, which means "night crow," is a fine description of this bird's general look and size. Night-herons are large and often look dark, especially the young, and they are stocky and short-tailed like a crow. But that is where the similarity ends. These widespread herons spend much of the day sleeping, hidden from view in dense trees; they emerge to hunt at night. Once you learn the *waaak!* call, you will hear this common resident flying by at night or in the early morning. Night-herons thrive in fishing ports, and trees near harbors often have big patches of whitewash beneath them, revealing the heron's roost. Colusa NWR is a great place to see roosting birds; large numbers are sometimes found in the Sierra Valley.

Adult elegantly plumaged, white and gray with black crown and back. Stout black bill and short yellowish legs.

Juvenile stocky, brown with white teardrops in plumage. Two-year-old bird more similar to adult, but duller, browner.

Osprey

Pandion haliaetus

L 22" | **WS** 64"

A fish specialist, the Osprey dives talons first into the water to take prey. The outer wing can rotate to get the bird and its large fish out of the water and into the air. Ospreys are uncommon in most of California, but more numerous in the far north. Many are found in the Klamath Valley in the warmer months; Ospreys are apparently spreading in central California, and they have recently nested in the port of San Francisco. Many Ospreys winter in Central or South America, but some remain in central and southern California. Listen for their loud, repetitive whistled calls.

In flight, very long-winged with slight crook at bend of wing. White body and wing linings, face with obvious dark stripe through eyes.

Perched shows long wings, but oddly pigeon-headed look, as if head too small. White underparts and head, with bold dark stripe through eyes.

Turkey Vulture

Cathartes aura

L 28" | **WS** 68.5"

The Turkey Vulture uses its vision and its highly developed sense of smell to find carrion. Present throughout California over the entire year, retreating only from cold and snow, this is often the most common raptor in the sky. Sizeable numbers migrate through the state, especially down the Kern Valley in fall. The big, broad wings of vultures can resemble Golden Eagle, but the vulture looks headless at a distance. The Turkey Vulture also teeters as it flies, and holds its wings higher above the horizontal than Golden Eagle.

Big and dark. The horizontal body of perched birds resembles turkey. Naked red head and yellow bill, both dark in younger birds.

In flight, long broad wings with "fingers" at tip. Wings are held up in shallow V; teeters side to side as it flies. Looks almost headless.

California Condor

Gymnogyps californianus

L 50″ | **WS** 109″

Condors have been part of the California landscape for millennia; huge fossil condors have been recovered from the La Brea Tar Pits in downtown Los Angeles. The California Condor nearly suffered the same fate as its prehistoric cousins. In 1987, concerned biologists captured the last twenty-two wild condors for captive breeding. This ongoing program has been very successful, and there are now more than 400 California Condors, most of which have been released into the wild. Lead poisoning is a significant obstacle to recovery. Reintroduced condors can now be seen in Pinnacles National Park and the Big Sur area, where they sometimes descend to the coast to feed on dead marine mammals.

Huge, with many "fingers" on wing tip. Adult black with white triangular patches on underwing. This bird is marked for tracking and study by biologists.

Huge blackish immature much bigger than Turkey Vulture. Dark head; pale area on underwing not as distinct in flight as adult's.

Golden Eagle

Aquila chrysaetos

L 30" | **WS** 80"

The Golden Eagle hunts mammals in savanna or grassland habitats and mountainous country, taking jackrabbits, ground squirrels, or even larger prey. Year-round residents, these eagles attain their highest population densities anywhere in the Diablo Range east of the Bay area. Typical of very large raptors, they take five or six years to attain adult plumage. Younger birds have variable amounts of white on the tail base and the base of the primaries, but not in the wing pit as in the Bald Eagle.

Huge raptor. Large head with menacing bill, contrasting golden nape.

Adult in flight brown with dark tail and gleaming golden nape. Like a massive Turkey Vulture with large, feathered head.

Bald Eagle

Haliaeetus leucocephalus

L 33″ | **WS** 80″

The Bald Eagle, our famous national symbol, is also a conservation success story. Numbers have bounced back since the ban on the pesticide DDT, which accumulated in the Bald Eagle and other top predators, making their eggs fragile and brittle. Now Bald Eagles are rebounding strongly, though they are not as common in California as in many other states. Primarily a fish-eater, this eagle can be found nearly anywhere there is open water. Bald Eagles are most abundant at far northern sites, such as Tule Lake and the Klamath Basin. Eagles take many years to mature; in the puzzlingly variable immature stages, look for white in the "wingpits" of the young Bald Eagle to distinguish it from a Golden Eagle.

Unique adult huge and dark with white head and tail; large, bright yellow beak and legs.

In flight, long, broad, rectangular wings.

Young start out brown with speckled white on wing linings, belly, and tail. Older immatures are white-headed with Osprey-like dark stripe.

White-tailed Kite

Elanus leucurus

L 20″ | **WS** 52″

This is one of our most graceful raptors in its shape, movements, and subtly beautiful plumage. Kites are often seen hovering with head pointed into the breeze, waiting to dive on an unsuspecting vole. California's White-tailed Kites are year-round residents, widespread in grasslands, agricultural areas, and savannas; some birds from the interior may move to the coast in winter. Populations are highest during periodic rodent outbreaks. In the nonbreeding season, kites often roost in groups of up to a hundred birds.

An elegant and slim raptor, with white body and head, gray upperparts, and black shoulders. Dark area around reddish eye makes face look serene.

Pointed wings, white body and tail, black shoulders, and dark patch on underside of wing obvious in flight.

Northern Harrier

Circus cyaneus

L 19" | **WS** 43"

Harriers hunt low over the ground, teetering side to side on wings held up in a shallow V. The owl-like disks around the eyes help focus sound; once prey has been seen or heard, the harrier turns and pounces. All Northern Harriers have a white rump patch, but the body plumage and size vary depending on age and sex; adult males are gray and much smaller than the big brown females. Uniquely among our hawks, male harriers may breed with more than one female, a system known as polygyny. Harriers are common year-round residents throughout California. The Central Valley National Wildlife Refuges in winter are good places to see the Northern Harrier.

In flight, holds wings in a shallow V. Adult male is blue-gray with paler underparts. All plumages have white rump.

Perched, the owl-like facial disks give a unique look. Very long wings. Females and young birds brown above, juveniles cinnamon below.

Sharp-shinned Hawk

Accipiter striatus

L 11.5" | **WS** 19"

A colloquial name for this quick little hawk is "blue bullet." The genus Accipiter is made up of fast, highly maneuverable bird hunters that surprise their prey and chase it down in flight. The rounded wings and long tails are good for tight turns and short bursts of speed. The "sharpie," the smallest of our Accipiters, tends to feed on smaller songbirds. Mainly a winter visitor in California, the Sharp-shinned Hawk also breeds uncommonly in dense conifer forests in the north and mountains. It can show up anywhere in migration and winter; a particularly good place to see this species is Hawk Hill in Marin County during fall, when many can move through on a single day. In addition to the smaller size, the shorter, more square-tipped tail is a good distinction from the larger Cooper's Hawk.

Adult rusty below with long, squarish tipped tail. Lacks blackish cap of Cooper's Hawk.

Long, square-tipped tail, small head with large eyes. Immature brownish above, uneven streaking below.

Cooper's Hawk

Accipiter cooperii

L 15″ | **WS** 30″

This is a common year-round resident of California, frequenting backyards with bird feeders. An efficient hunter of doves, it appears to be increasing in urban areas. If you see an Accipiter in summer in a suburban area, it is almost certainly a Cooper's Hawk. With practice, this species is identified from the Sharp-shinned Hawk by its consistently larger size, larger head, and longer and more round-tipped tail. The white tail tip is also broader and more noticeable. In adults, the blackish cap gives the Cooper's away. Near the nest, gives a dry *chek chek chek*… call.

Adult rusty below; outer tail feather noticeably shorter than rest of long tail. Contrasting blackish cap.

Longer, round-tipped tail and larger head than Sharp-shinned. Immature brownish above with crisp streaking below.

Red-shouldered Hawk

Buteo lineatus

L 20″ | **WS** 40″

With its strongly banded black and white wings and tail, the Red-shouldered could also have been called the "zebra hawk." Common residents west of the Sierra, the California populations of this widely distributed bird are colorful, rich reddish and bold black and white in adults, with immatures not much less striking. An adaptable bird, found anywhere with taller trees, including suburban backyards, where Red-shoulders perch and wait for snakes, lizards, and other prey. Often seen perching on roadside electrical wires and posts. The Red-shoulder is a particularly noisy hawk, with a repeated gull-like *keeahh keeahh keeahh....*

Adult bulky, with barred rusty underparts, head, and shoulders. Wing and tail boldly zebra-striped.

Flies with quick flaps and a glide. Strongly banded wings and tail, reddish wing linings and shoulder. Backlit wing shows pale crescent at base of primaries.

Brownish immature streaked below with reddish on shoulders. Strongly banded wings and tail.

Red-tailed Hawk

Buteo jamaicensis

L 20″ | **WS** 48.5″

This is one of the most successful and widespread raptors on the continent. A common resident in California, populations of this bird are augmented in winter by migrants from the north. This is one of the most variable hawks, with notable differences between immatures and adults and considerable individual variation. Typical birds are pale, but there are also dark individuals and rufous, or intermediate birds in which rusty-brown replaces the white plumage. This hawk spends much of its time soaring in search of food. The call is an aggressive-sounding *keeargggggg* scream.

Large, thick-set hawk. Brown adult mottled pale above, with darker head, pale breast, and noticeable reddish tail.

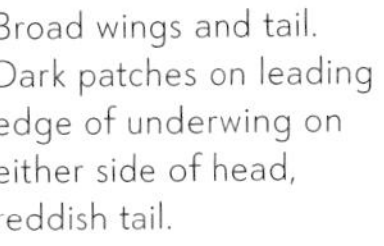

Broad wings and tail. Dark patches on leading edge of underwing on either side of head, reddish tail.

Immature brownish, with banded brown tail. Like adult, shows dark patches on leading edge of wing. Pale breast contrast with darker belly.

Variable. Dark adult chocolate-brown with red tail.

Swainson's Hawk

Buteo swainsoni

L 20.5" | **WS** 50"

Raptors of open grassland and agricultural areas, Swainson's Hawk feeds on grasshoppers, dragonflies, and other large insects caught on the wing, supplementing their diet with rodents during the breeding season. Breeding populations are highest in the Central Valley. They are highly migratory, with most heading to Argentina in winter; curiously, some remain to winter in California's Central Valley. In the spring, numbers can be seen moving north through the desert along the mountains. Often seen sitting on the ground. Variable, with an uncommon dark morph; the long and pointed wing shape always aids in identification.

Pale adult with dark breast and white underparts. Always shows long wings extending past tail. Uniform dark above, face with white throat and base of bill.

In flight, slim, long, and somewhat pointed wings, often held up in slight dihedral. Immature streaked below. Darker flight feathers contrast with paler wing linings.

Ferruginous Hawk

Buteo regalis

L 24.5" | **WS** 54"

The Ferruginous Hawk is a species of the wide-open Great Plains during the breeding season. In winter, some migrate to California's arid short grass habitats and open agricultural land. They hunt mammals such as ground squirrels, and often take larger prey than the Red-tailed Hawk; not only is the Ferruginous slightly larger, but its larger gape allows it to swallow bigger prey. Like the Swainson's Hawk, the Ferruginous perches on the ground. Adults of the uncommon dark morph have chocolate-brown bodies, but the pinkish white tail is similar to that of pale birds.

Large, colorful hawk, rusty above and whitish below with darker "pants." Long, drooping gape makes it look unhappy.

In flight, a large, pale hawk with long and somewhat pointed wings. Pale adults with whitish pink tail, dark comma-shaped marks at bend of wing. Immature with darker legs, more streaks below, and darker tail.

Sandhill Crane

Grus canadensis

L 47″ | **WS** 78.5″

Big and long-necked, cranes are sometimes confused with herons, but unlike herons, cranes fly with neck extended and an odd flapping style, with the upstroke appearing faster than the downstroke. At close range, they show a distinctive reddish crown. The gray plumage is often stained rusty. Birds of grasslands, fields, and wetland edges, Sandhill Cranes breed on northern tundra and in the taiga, visiting California only in the winter. Their strongholds are the Central Valley refuges, where they congregate in good numbers. Cranes have a loop in their windpipe that allows them to produce loud, rolling bugling calls, often given in flight, *krr–rraannk*.

A huge, grayish crane with long neck and long black bill and legs. Bare red crown patch. Unusual shape with "bustle" of feathers over tail.

Neck outstretched in flight, unlike herons; uniformly dark gray.

Ridgway's Rail

Rallus obsoletus

L 14" | **WS** 18.5"

This shy bird is a threatened species, restricted to the salt marshes of San Francisco Bay and wetlands in the Imperial and Colorado Valleys and coastal southern California. The best places to see this reclusive bird are salt marshes in San Francisco Bay during winter high tides; the Palo Alto Baylands are a favorite spot. The Ridgway's is much larger than the similarly shaped Virginia Rail. Ridgway's loud calls include a *kek kek kek kek* and *kek kek karrrr.*

A large rail with long, thick orange bill. Warm cinnamon neck sides and slightly more grayish face, dull barring on flanks.

Virginia Rail

Rallus limicola

L 9″ | **WS** 14″

This widespread resident is found in dense cattail and tule marshes throughout California; its abundance and distribution is uncertain because of its secretive nature. The key to seeing rails is to visit appropriate habitat very early in the morning or late in the evening, watching the muddy edges. Highly vocal, particularly early in the breeding season, the male gives a series of grunts that decrease in pitch, as well as a *kik kik kik kidik kidik kidik*. Females give a *chi chi chi chi trrrrrr*. Other mysterious marsh sounds may be produced by this rail, which often calls at night.

Gray cheek and bolder black and white flank barring are conspicuous.

Sora

Porzana carolina

L 8.5" | **WS** 14"

The smallest and chunkiest of our rails, the short-billed Sora, a widespread breeder and resident, is also the most frequently encountered. It lives in freshwater habitats such as tule and cattail marshes or wetlands with shrubby edges. More often heard than seen, but this shy rail sometimes emerges onto the mud at the edge of a marsh early in the morning or late in the evening. The call is a distinctive whinny that slows and descends in pitch at the end. The whinny is sometimes preceded by a series of questioning *pweep? pweep? pweep?* notes.

A small, compact rail with gray neck and black face that contrasts with short, chicken-like yellowish bill.

Common Gallinule

Gallinula galeata

L 13″ | **WS** 23″

This is a chicken-like water bird whose behavior is intermediate between that of a coot and a rail: It swims like a coot, but sometimes retreats into thick vegetation like a rail. When swimming, it shows a high rear end and long tail with bright white undertail coverts. Found mainly in the southern half of the state, gallinules are common in parts of the Central Valley, with notable winter concentrations at Gray Lodge Wildlife Area. Gives a variety of clucking calls and a distinctive series of laughing cackles.

Stocky, dark gray bird with red and yellow bill and forehead shield; long yellow legs and toes. White flank line and undertail coverts.

Flat-backed with colorful red and yellow bill and shield; white undertail coverts and flank stripe. Immature brownish with dull bill.

American Coot

Fulica americana

L 16″ | **WS** 24″

A common resident throughout California, coot numbers are highest in winter, when birds from farther north migrate to the state's natural wetlands and park and golf course ponds. Though they flock in the non-breeding season, coots are pugnacious birds, often fighting with each other. In the water, they tip up or dive briefly for aquatic vegetation; they also graze on lawns near water. The feet are not webbed like a duck's, but have lobes on each toe to propel them through the water. Calls are puffing and sputtering notes, *pfft pfft* or *prrr-fft, prr-fft*....

Stocky, with domed back, largely white bill and forehead shield. Lead-gray body, blackish head and neck.

Rotund, dark gray body, largely white bill and shield, tiny tail. Legs greenish, toes with flattened lobes.

Black Oystercatcher

Haematopus bachmani

L 17.5″ | **WS** 32″

The Black Oystercatcher is a bird of rocky coasts, where it hunts for shellfish (though not specifically oysters) at low tide. It is often found with Surfbirds or Black Turnstones. Black Oystercatchers are common along the entire California coast and on the Channel Islands, some venturing into the central part of San Francisco Bay. Usually seen as pairs or family groups, but larger groups form at high tide. The immature is browner and has a dusky tip to the bill. Loud and raucous, the call is a single *kleep!* The display includes a long series of yelping whistles, often given by both members of a pair, often in flight *wheep wheep wheep weepeteeteeteeteetee....*

Big and thickset. Dark brown with black head and neck. Bill looks like carrot on face. Thick, dull pink legs and gorgeous yellow eye with orange orbital ring.

Black-necked Stilt

Himantopus mexicanus

L 14.5″ | **WS** 28″

Among our waterbirds, the stilts have the longest legs in proportion to their body size. Males are black-backed and females are browner. Juveniles can show a scaly pattern on the brownish upperparts. Common residents of shallow wetlands across the state, including salt evaporation ponds in the San Francisco Bay area, stilts can be seen at the Palo Alto Baylands and wetlands in San Diego Bay. They forage by picking food from the surface of the water or mud with the very finely tipped bill rather than by probing. The common voice is a nasal barking *pweek pweek*… repeated almost incessantly.

Slim black and white shorebird with pink stilts for legs; white spot above eye creates perky facial expression.

Female similar to male, but brownish black back.

American Avocet

Recurvirostra americana

L 18″ | **WS** 28″

Swishing their uniquely upturned bill from side to side, avocets forage by straining small food particles from the water. The female's bill is more strongly curved, allowing the sexes to forage in different water depths. Avocets are common residents in California, their numbers increasing in winter as birds arrive from the north and east. Flocks congregate at sites such as South San Francisco Bay and Owens Lake. Flight calls are strident barks, *kwiip! kwiip! kwiip!*

Unique bill, more strongly upcurved in female. Thickset body with long neck and gray legs. Black and white body with rusty head and neck during breeding.

Male with less upturned bill. In winter, black and white body and grayish neck.

Black-bellied Plover

Pluvialis squatarola

L 11″ | **WS** 23″

The Black-bellied Plover breeds in the Arctic. We see them in California as migrants and in winter, although immature birds sometimes remain in the south during their first summer. Immature and winter birds are mainly grayish; later in spring, a few will look quite spectacular with their black breast and face. At all seasons, they have a black patch on the "wing pits" unlike any other shorebird. They feed by locating food visually on the surface of the mud. The voice is a pleasant, loud whistle *Fee-aa-weeuuuu*. Black-bellied Plovers function as sentinel species on the mudflat, sounding the alarm and taking flight before other, less wary shorebirds.

Breeding plumage striking, with black face, neck, and breast contrasting with whitish crown and hind neck and checkered back and wings. Female more brownish.

In winter, pot-bellied, grayish brown above and paler below; stout peg-like black bill and large dark eye. Juvenile crisply speckled above.

In flight, shows a large black area on the "wingpit"; whitish tail and bold white wing stripe.

Snowy Plover

Charadrius nivosus

L 6″ | **WS** 13″

The Snowy Plover occupies two different habitats in California, sandy beaches and flat salt ponds, where the pale upperparts blend in to the background; these birds even crouch in shallow depressions to keep from casting a shadow. Since people love beaches, too, the plovers have lost a lot of breeding habitat; signs and fencing are now put up in an effort to keep people and dogs out of nesting and roosting areas. Look for this uncommon bird at Devereux Slough in Santa Barbara or on the beach north of Half Moon Bay. Typically very quiet, but gives soft *pip* notes.

Small, compact plover with thin black bill and dark legs. Breeding plumage with warm brown crown and black mask, forehead, and spurs on breast side.

Nonbreeding birds with black bill, dark legs, dark breast spurs, and narrow white ring around neck.

Semipalmated Plover

Charadrius semipalmatus

L 7″ | **WS** 14″

The odd name name of this bird refers to the small palmations—webs between the toes—a feature that few birders get close enough to see. A small banded plover, darker above and thicker-billed than the Snowy, the Semipalmated Plover is a bird of mudflats, where it often forages at the edge of mixed flocks, looking for food to pick from the water or mud. Sometimes they wiggle their feet to liquefy soft mud and get invertebrates to move to the surface. This is a northern breeder that winters in California, where it is commonly found on any mudflat, such as those at Arcata Bay or in Foster City, San Mateo. A very vocal plover, it often gives its presence away with a mellow whistled *tuu–wheep!*

Small, stocky plover with orange legs and thick orange-based bill. Wet-sand brown above, with white collar; breeding bird has black breast band and facial markings.

Juvenile and non-breeding birds lack black on face; brown breast band contrasts with wide white collar. Orange legs, dark bill; juvenile scaly looking above.

Killdeer

Charadrius vociferus

L 9" | **WS** 18.5"

The Killdeer is not the most abundant of our plovers, but it may well be the most frequently encountered. It is a year-round resident in California, where it occupies open habitats in agricultural, suburban, and urban areas. Any flat gravelly area, even the edge of a parking lot, can be a breeding site for a Killdeer. If you find a nest, Killdeer, like other shorebirds, will feign a broken wing, screaming raucously and spreading its orange tail to lead you away from the eggs. The adult's double breast bands are a key field mark; downy young have only one band. The scientific name says it all: this is a vociferous bird, whose screeching *deer deer deer* or *Kil-deer Kil-deer* inspired its common name.

Medium-size plover with very long tail and long body. Tell-tale double bands on breast. Rusty tail base; complex face pattern often gives sad appearance.

Willet

Tringa semipalmata

L 14.5″ | **WS** 27″

Named for one of its calls, the Willet is a common species in California during its winter non-breeding season. Migrants move as early as July to the coast and estuaries to spend the winter feeding on mudflats and sandy beaches. Look for them on the Hayward shoreline or around San Diego Bay, where they can be common. The voice is a harsh and rolling *krrii riii riii!* In the breeding season, sings a repeated *pill-will-willet* often in flight.

Nonbreeding bird is a bulky, long-necked, gray shorebird. Stout, straight gray-based bill and medium length gray legs. White around eyes looks like it is wearing glasses.

Bold black and white wing pattern in flight. Barred and speckled plumage in breeding season.

Spotted Sandpiper

Actitis macularius

L 7.5″ | **WS** 15″

Spotted Sandpipers are unusual sandpipers: they do not breed in the far north, they don't tend to flock, and they are often along rocky streams rather than out on mudflats. Except when migrating, they fly low over water with bursts of shallow fluttering wing beats followed by glides, quite unlike any other sandpiper. Spotted Sandpipers breed in the Sierra, and small numbers migrate and winter mainly the coast. A key to identification is the constant bobbing of the rear part of the body and tail. The call is a sharp *pee tweet tweet.*

Constantly bobbing; a small and long-tailed shorebird. In breeding plumage, has orange-based bill and bold spotting below.

Tail extends past folded wings. Nonbreeding birds warm buffy above with white underparts.

Wandering Tattler

Tringa incana

L 11″ | **WS** 20.5″

Like the Spotted Sandpiper, the Wandering Tattler is a tail-bobber. Solitary and sparsely distributed, this species is nearly always found in coastal rocky habitats, usually at the periphery of gatherings of other "rock pipers" such as the Black Turnstone and Surfbird, though it does not actively fly and flock with those species. Tattlers can be found in any rocky area on the coast, including jetties in harbors with riprap, such as Los Angeles. In some ways the tattler looks like a short-legged and bulky yellowlegs, with the gray color and facial features of a Willet. The voice is a hollow and quavering *pipipipipiri*.

A mid-size, stocky, but long shorebird, with stout bill and yellow legs. Bobs on rocks. In breeding, plumage barred grayish below.

Nonbreeding plumage gray with yellow legs. Face and bill recall a miniature Willet, but found on rocks, where it tends to bob its body.

Greater Yellowlegs

Tringa melanoleuca

L 13.5" | **WS** 27.5"

The Greater and Lesser Yellowlegs are among the trickiest of bird identifications, and in California they are not often seen together for comparison of size. The key points are the length, thickness, and color of the bill and the overall size of the bird. The bill of the Greater Yellowlegs is longer than the head; it is thicker than that of the Lesser, and tends to have a gray base against which the dark nostril stands out. The Greater Yellowlegs is much larger than the Lesser. Breeding on boreal ponds and in bogs, Greater Yellowegs move south for the nonbreeding season, when they can be found on vegetated mudflats, pond edges, or shallow wetlands. This is the more common yellowlegs in California. Greater Yellowlegs often call when they fly, usually three or four strident notes *tew tew TEW!*

Relatively large shorebird with long neck and bill and bright yellow legs. Bill looks longer than the head; often pale-based, so dark nostril stands out.

Non-breeding and juvenile birds whitish below with obscure streaking on neck. Long bill pale-based, so that nostril stands out. Yellow legs.

Lesser Yellowlegs

Tringa flavipes

L 10" | **WS** 27"

The Lesser Yellowlegs is at best an uncommon migrant and winterer in California. It is separated from the more common Greater, our "default" yellowlegs, by its smaller size and the bill characters: the bill is about the length of the head, pin-thin, and typically entirely black. Rather than mudflats or beach, Lesser Yellowlegs seek out pond edges and shallow marshes with vegetation. Bolsa Chica Preserve and Don Edwards NWR in Alviso are good places to look. The one- or two-syllable calls *teep teep* are less forceful than the Greater's.

Smaller and slimmer than Greater Yellowlegs; bill thin, darker at base; and about as long as head. Yellow legs; breeding plumage barred above and below.

Both yellowlegs have white rumps and long yellow legs that trail behind the pale tail. Lesser is smaller with thinner, shorter bill.

Whimbrel

Numenius phaeopus

L 17″ | **WS** 32.5″

The Whimbrel has the long, downcurved bill of all curlews. It is shorter-billed and stockier-bodied than the Long-billed Curlew, and has a distinctly patterned dark crown with a pale central stripe. Whimbrels feed among rocks, on sand, and on the drier upper reaches of mudflats. This Arctic breeder is a long-distance migrant; most of the Whimbrels seen in California are on the way to wintering grounds in Peru and Chile, but numbers remain to winter in the state, often on beaches with adjacent rocky areas. Look for them from Crescent City Harbor to the Tijuana Slough. Call a hollow-sounding, rapid *quiquiquiquiqui*.

Large shorebird with stout, decurved bill. Brown body with noticeably darker head stripes, short and thick grayish legs. In flight, brownish gray, including underwings.

Long-billed Curlew

Numenius americanus

L 22.5″ | **WS** 30″

This curlew has an incredibly long bill; up close, a fleshy blob is visible at the tip, the bird's primary sensory organ for finding food. Long-billed Curlews probe the mud or pick from the surface, using the bill like a tweezer. Smaller and shorter-billed birds in the flocks are the males. A breeder on the Great Plains and Great Basin grasslands, this species migrates to estuaries and agricultural fields and grasslands in the Central Valley during the nonbreeding season. Look for it in the Antelope Valley in the south, Palo Alto Baylands, or Hayward shoreline in the Bay area. Seems to say its name as it flies, *cur-leee*.

Large shorebird with very long decurved bill ending in a fleshy tip. Dull face pattern with no head stripes; eye stands out on pale face. Warm cinnamon tones below, particularly on underwing in flight.

Marbled Godwit

Limosa fedoa

L 17.5″ | **WS** 31.5″

Often found with Willets and Long-billed Curlews, the Marbled Godwit resembles the curlew in size and plumage, but has a long, straight or slightly upturned bill. Big, long-legged, and long billed-birds are the females, which feed in deeper water than the males. The bill base varies individually from pink to orange. Godwits commonly roost on rocky headlands at high tide. They feed on sandy beaches or by probing tidal mudflats in estuaries or bays. They are less frequent in the north of the state, but Moss Landing, Radio Road Ponds in Redwood Shores, Hayward Shoreline, Bolsa Chica, Mission Bay, and the Salton Sea are great places to observe this species during migration and winter. Typically silent, but has a loud, gull-like *kyaaaK!* call.

Large shorebird with long, slightly upturned, strongly bicolored bill. Body brown with cinnamon tones, particularly on underparts.

Breeding plumage barred on body, less cinnamon; bill often darker.

In flight, cinnamon underwings are similar to Long-billed Curlew, but upturned bill clearly different.

Red Knot

Calidris canutus

L 9.5" | **WS** 21"

Breeding largely in Siberia, the Red Knot is an uncommon and local migrant and winterer on tidal mudflats from the Bay Area southwards, often flocking with Short-billed Dowitchers or Dunlins. Look for it in the Bay Area at the Hayward Shoreline, Shell Bar in Foster City, Bolsa Chica in the Los Angeles area, and at the San Diego River mouth. This species is usually seen in gray winter plumage, but by late April many can be in their gorgeous breeding colors. Typically silent.

Stunning in breeding plumage, rusty face and underparts with white vent, white and rust spangled upperparts. Thickset body, bill almost as long as head, short dark legs.

In nonbreeding plumage, gray-bodied, paler below with gray spots and chevrons on flanks. Stocky with short greenish legs, pale grayish rump in flight.

Ruddy Turnstone

Arenaria interpres

L 7″ | **WS** 21″

Ruddy Turnstones breed in the high Arctic, then migrate to coastlines all around the world. They occur in coastal California as singles or in small flocks, and are rare inland, though regularly encountered at the Salton Sea. The preferred habitat is mudflats adjacent to rocky or sandy areas. The Ruddy is much more likely to be found in estuaries than the more coastal Black Turnstone. Great places to look include Tomales Bay, Foster City Shell Bar, Moss Landing, and Bolsa Chica. Not always vocal, but may give a trilling *tr-tr-tu-tu*… in flight.

Breeding plumage gorgeous rusty and black upperparts, complex pattern on head and neck. Bill flat-topped and pointed; bright orange legs.

Stocky, short-legged, with pointed and flat-topped bill. Nonbreeding plumage with brownish body, white below with orange legs. Pale "saddlebags" on sides of dark neck.

Black Turnstone

Arenaria melanocephala

L 9″ | **WS** 21″

Black Turnstones are one of the classic rock-loving shorebirds of our coasts. These "rock pipers" feed in the splash zone, often with Surfbirds and sometimes with Black Oystercatchers or Whimbrels. The Black Turnstone uses its bill to flip through drying algal mats to uncover food. Black Turnstones breed in coastal Alaska, and migrate to winter primarily in California. One can find them anywhere on the coast, but Bodega Bay is especially good. They give a distinctive quavering rattle in flight.

Stocky, short-legged with pointed and flat-topped bill. Blackish brown with white underparts, unmarked flanks. Breeding plumage with white patch at bill base.

Blackish with white belly, unmarked white flanks. In flight has calico pattern of white and black, including white rump. Dull reddish legs, flat-topped pointed bill.

Surfbird

Calidris virgata

L 10″ | **WS** 26″

The Surfbird and the Black Turnstone are both classic "rock pipers," shorebirds that are especially typical of coastal rocky habitats, foraging in the surf zone and gathering into larger flocks to sleep at high tide. Surfbirds breed along rocky creeks in Alaska and the Yukon, and spend the nonbreeding season on the Pacific Coast as far south as Chile. Common on California's rocky coasts and jetties, the Surfbird is less likely to venture into estuaries than the Black Turnstone. Look for it on Humboldt Bay jetties and at Point Reyes, Pescadero State Beach, the Playa del Rey pier, and the San Diego River mouth. Generally silent.

Mid-size bulky shorebird with short greenish yellow legs. Nonbreeding plumage the color of wet rocks, white underparts with spotted flanks. Stocky peg-like bill with orange base to mandible.

Orange base to mandible on peg-like bill, yellowish legs. Stocky mid-size shorebird; in breeding plumage, upperparts with rust centers, beautifully spotted and barred below.

Sanderling

Calidris alba

L 7.5″ | **WS** 13.5″

This pale winter bird is what most people think of when they hear the name "sandpiper." Truly fond of sandy beaches, Sanderlings chase the retreating waves, pecking at food for an instant before running back to drier sand as the next wave breaks. They leave California for the high Arctic by late May, but return to the wintering grounds by late July. Look for them anywhere on California's beaches. Usually silent, the call is a flat *kiip*.

Nonbreeding birds very pale gray above with blackish bend of wing and white upward spur immediately in front of wing. Mid-length black bill and black legs.

Breeding male beautiful brick-red on breast and upperparts, white underparts. This plumage held only briefly.

Dunlin

Calidris alpina

L 7" | **WS** 14.5"

The Dunlin is another Arctic-breeding shorebird that winters in California. It arrives much later in fall than most other shorebirds, typically not until late September. More common in northern and central California than the south, Dunlins winter commonly in the Central Valley and along major estuaries. Arcata Bay, Bodega Bay, Tomales Bay, and various sites around San Francisco Bay can hold thousands in winter. In years of high rainfall, more Dunlin may winter on the coast than in the Central Valley. They feed mainly on mudflats or the muddy edges of flooded fields. The flight call is a rolling *prreeeep*, longer than the calls of peeps.

Mid-size with long, black, down-curved bill and black legs. Dusky above and on breast and head, white below; dull face pattern makes beady black eye stand out.

In breeding plumage, rusty back and crown, pale face and neck with fine streaking, bold black belly batch. Long, downcurved black bill and black legs.

Least Sandpiper

Calidris minutilla

L 6.5″ | **WS** 16.5″

The smallest of our sandpipers is a dark shorebird with pale legs and a dark breast. It forages on the dry upper areas of mudflats, where it crouches in the sparse vegetation. Breeds in boreal wetlands, and migrates to California for the winter, where it is common in coastal estuaries and the Central and Imperial Valleys; large numbers congregate in Arcata Bay and at sites in San Francisco Bay. The flight call is a rolling and excited *preeep*, shorter and less strident than the call of the Dunlin.

Our smallest sandpiper, with a fine-tipped, slightly decurved bill and yellowish legs. Nonbreeding birds dusky on head, back, and breast; white below with bold whitish eye ring.

Small; fine-tipped droopy bill and yellowish legs. Juvenile bright cinnamon above, white stripes on back and scapulars, slightly streaked breast.

Western Sandpiper

Calidris mauri

L 6″ | **WS** 12″

Larger and generally paler-breasted than the Least Sandpiper, this species shows a long, droopy, Dunlin-like bill and dark legs. Western Sandpipers breed in Alaska and migrate to both coasts, though they are much more abundant along the Pacific Coast. Especially in spring, a huge proportion of the world's population migrates through San Francisco Bay: in late April, hundreds of thousands may be present at any one time. They can be viewed at higher tides from Hayward Shoreline, Palo Alto Baylands, Coyote Hills, and many other sites. Smaller but still sizeable numbers occur elsewhere on tidal mudflats and in the Central Valley. The flight call is a short, weak *tcheet*, without the trilling quality of the Least Sandpiper.

Small shorebird with long, droopy black bill and blackish legs. Juvenile gleaming white below including breast, and warm above with rusty scapulars. Non-breeding birds similar but dull grayish above.

Small sandpiper with droopy bill, shorter on males, and blackish legs. Breeding plumage with rusty cap, cheeks, and scapulars. White below, with arrowhead streaks on breast and flanks.

Pectoral Sandpiper

Calidris melanotos

L 8.5″ | **WS** 17″

The Pectoral Sandpiper looks like an overgrown Least Sandpiper, but it has a distinctive brown-streaked breast band that ends abruptly at the line between the breast and belly. Pectoral Sandpipers forage on the shallow edges of vegetated wetlands or in wet grassy fields. An Arctic breeder that migrates south to winter in Argentina, they occur in California mainly as autumn migrants. Good places to look include the Centerville wetlands and Elk River mouth in the north, Don Edwards NWR in southern San Francisco Bay, and along the Los Angeles River. Silent while foraging, but in flight it utters a low-pitched, rolling *pruuuup*.

Streaky brown, mid-size shorebird with yellowish legs. Breast streaking stops in abrupt straight line where it meets the white belly. Nonbreeding birds dull brownish gray above.

Juvenile with rusty scapulars and white "suspender" lines.

Wilson's Snipe

Gallinago delicata

L 11.5" | **WS** 17"

The description of an impossible task as a "snipe hunt" is based on this bird's extreme stealth and explosive, twisting flight. The word "sniper" was originally applied to hunters so skilled that they could shoot a snipe. This secretive bird is often found hiding in vegetation along ponds, rivers, and other freshwater habitats, including flooded fields. Easier to see on the breeding grounds in northeast California, where they perform "winnowing" displays—the vibrating tail feathers create a distinctive "hollow" sound as the bird dives through the air. Snipe migrate and winter throughout the state, with significant numbers at Central Valley refuges such as Sacramento NWR. They may perch on a post and give a syncopated call *kit-kit-kit*....

Mid-size rotund shorebird with very long, straight bill. Eyes high up on the head, recalling face of a jackrabbit. Bold creamy white stripes on back.

Long-billed Dowitcher

Limnodromus scolopaceus

L 11″ | **WS** 19″

The two dowitchers are notoriously difficult to identify unless their distinctive voices are heard. In breeding plumage, the Long-billed tends to be darker, more consistently rufous throughout the underparts, and less variably patterned on the upperparts and flanks. Bill length overlaps widely with the Short-billed. Long-billeds breed in Alaska and migrate and winter across California, including inland. This dowitcher usually keeps to freshwater sites, so birds wintering in the Central Valley are Long-billeds. They are found on pond edges, in flooded fields, and along the edges of shallow lakes and marshes. The call is a single high-pitched *keek!*, sometimes hard to pick out in mixed shorebird flocks.

Plump-bodied, mid-size shorebird with very long straight bill, medium-length greenish legs. In breeding plumage, rusty below to vent, flanks show narrow black bar and white tip. Upperparts dar with crisp white feather tips.

Nonbreeding birds brownish gray, including breast, with barred flanks. Long straight bill can be more than twice length of head.

Fall juvenile with cinnamon-edged upperparts, dark-centered tertials with cinnamon to cream fringes. Warm wash on flanks and breast.

Short-billed Dowitcher

Limnodromus griseus

L 11″ | **WS** 19″

The two dowitchers are among the most vexing bird identifications in California. The key is their distinctive calls. The Short-billed gives a low-pitched, rapidly delivered *tlu-tu-tu* that can recall the voice of one of the yellowlegs, very different from the higher-pitched single-syllable call of the Long-bill. Short-billed Dowitchers in breeding plumage are brighter and more golden above than Long-bills and often paler and more pinkish orange below, with a rather variable pattern of spotting or barring on the breast and flanks. Often there is considerable white on the belly. Short-billed Dowitchers prefer brackish or saltwater habitats, and are seen on tidal mudflats in migration and winter. Common at Arcata Marsh, the Palo Alto Baylands, Hayward Shoreline, Bolsa Chica, and San Diego NWR.

Plump-bodied, mid-size shorebird with long bill with slightly drooping tip, greenish legs. In breeding plumage, pinkish orange below mixed with white, variably patterned flanks, often spotted. Upperparts golden-rust, usually without white tips.

Nonbreeding birds grayish, bill usually less than twice the length of head, often with droop at tip. Paler and less barred than Long-billed; listen for call.

Fall juvenile brightly colored, with extensive orange tone to breast and flanks. Upperparts strongly marked rusty, tertials with complex internal markings.

Wilson's Phalarope

Phalaropus tricolor

L 19″ | **WS** 17″

Wilson's is the only phalarope found inland rather than out at sea. This species breeds throughout the interior West, including eastern California, and migrates to southern South America for the winter. Females do not stay at their nests, leaving breeding areas as early as late June. Males remain to incubate the eggs and hatchlings are left to feed and care for themselves. All Wilson's of both sexes have passed through California by mid-September. This phalarope is particularly fond of hyper-saline lakes, and tens of thousands can be found on Mono Lake in late summer. The salt ponds of South San Francisco Bay are also a good place to see this bird. Seldom heard away from the breeding areas.

A shorebird that swims. Breeding female is amazing, chestnut and gray above, with gray crown, dark eye stripe that blends to chestnut neck sides.

Long thin bill. Nonbreeding birds pale gray with weak face pattern, long, pointed rear end when swimming.

Red-necked Phalarope

Phalaropus lobatus

L 17.5" | **WS** 15"

The highly migratory Red-necked Phalarope is pelagic during the nonbreeding season, though in late August and early September small numbers of juvenile birds occur around southern San Francisco Bay and at other coastal sites. Offshore, this species is found with the larger, paler, thicker-billed Red Phalarope. Phalaropes feed while swimming, often spinning to create a vortex that concentrates small food particles. This Arctic breeder migrates south between late July and October and north from mid-April to late May. The call is a sharp *kiik*.

Swims, usually offshore. Breeding female stocky, thin pin-like bill. Head and neck dark gray with red neck sides; lead gray above with golden stripes.

Fall juvenile dark above with yellowish back stripe. Masked look, small pin-like black bill. More compact than Wilson's.

Tufted Puffin

Fratercula cirrhata

L 15″ | **WS** 29″

This is a bird that even non-birders recognize, from cereal box cartoons, wildlife shows, nature magazines, and calendars that invariably show a cute puffin with its huge and amazingly colorful bill. The Tufted is the only puffin with an entirely dark belly and, in the breeding season, long golden head tufts. In winter the bill is smaller and less colorful, and the white face patch is restricted to the area around the eyes. Tufted Puffins forage offshore, and are best seen by taking a pelagic boat trip. A colony of several hundred at the Farallon Islands can be visited in late summer on boats leaving Half Moon Bay or San Francisco.

Unique, black with gorgeous and massive orange red bill. Face white, ornamented with golden tufts.

Common Murre

Uria aalge

L 16" | **WS** 26.5"

Year-round residents in California, Common Murres are coastal seabirds that breed in large and dense colonies. They feed in colder water on small forage fishes, such as anchovies, and are much less common south of Morro Bay. Good places to see them during the breeding season include the Point Reyes Lighthouse, Devil's Slide north of Half Moon Bay, and the Farallon Islands, or on pelagic trips such as those from Half Moon Bay or Monterey. The male takes care of the single chick, which drops to the ocean from the cliffs before it is able to fly: the ocean is safer than the nesting islands, where predatory gulls abound. Offshore, the whistled calls of the young are answered by the throaty *arrrghhhh* of the father.

Long, loon-like bill is symmetrical and pointed. Breeding plumage black on back and head down to breast.

Black and white plumage, pointed bill. Nonbreeding birds with white face and dark stripe behind eye.

Pigeon Guillemot

Cepphus columba

L 12.5" | **WS** 22"

The dapper-looking Pigeon Guillemot breeds regularly on coastal cliffs and islets from the Oregon border to the Channel Islands. Unlike most of our birds, it moves north after breeding instead of south, with the majority migrating to British Columbia and Washington for winter. Look for guillemots on Santa Cruz and the Farallon Islands and at Point Reyes and Pigeon Point Lighthouse. The pale and speckled juveniles are often a mystery to observers, but their stout straight bills and the buoyancy with which they swim high in the water help identify them. Calls are high-pitched piping whistles.

Breeding plumage all black with white wing patch. Bright orange-red legs.

Duck-like profile, pointed bill. Non-breeding plumage black and white, dark head with white throat and cheeks, white wing patch.

Marbled Murrelet

Brachyramphus marmoratus

L 9.5″ | **WS** 9.5″

Marbled Murrelets can't decide if they are birds of the forest or the sea: they forage and spend most of their time on the ocean, but they nest high up on thick horizontal branches of old-growth trees, sadly, a diminishing habitat. The adults visit the nest only at night, so at the most you hear their gull-like *kleeer* as they fly over. Much more abundant in the northern part of California, Marbled Murrelets feed close to shore. The coast in Santa Cruz and Half Moon Bay are good places to seek them out.

Tiny alcid with small bill; nonbreeding plumage black and white with white half collar and white on scapulars.

Scripps's Murrelet

Synthliboramphus scrippsi

L 10" | **WS** 15"

All of the world's Scripps's Murrelets breed in California and nearby coastal Mexico, making this pelagic alcid a real specialty. Most are found in the Channel Islands, making a summertime visit to Santa Cruz Island a great chance to see this bird. In September and October, Scripps's Murrelets are regularly seen on pelagic birding trips, more frequently in years when there is warm water. These murrelets are almost always seen in pairs.

Tiny alcid with sharply pointed bill. Contrasting black above and white below, with white under wings. Face above the eyes is dark.

Rhinoceros Auklet

Cerorhinca monocerata

L 11″ | **WS** 24″

Although not nearly as ornately patterned, the Rhinoceros Auklet is closely related to the puffins. The pale "rhino horn" at the base of the bill is present only in the breeding season, and even then it can be quite difficult to see. This alcid nests in burrows on islands; management programs on the Farallon Islands and Año Nuevo Island provide artificial nesting burrows, which the auklets take to happily. Although sometimes seen from coastal points, this species is best found on pelagic birding trips, such as those out of Humboldt County, Half Moon Bay, and Monterey. Silent at sea, and typically solitary or in groups rarely larger than two or three birds.

Stocky, about the size of a football. Breeding bird has pale "rhino horn" at base of bill and two white plumes on face. In flight, shows pale belly.

Cassin's Auklet

Ptychoramphus aleuticus

L 9″ | **WS** 15″

This little island-nesting alcid has a boom-or-bust lifestyle. Cassin's Auklets do particularly well when krill is plentiful, but at other times of the year they forage on juvenile jellyfish and other sea creatures. When times are rich, they may breed twice in a season, but when food is scarce, they don't breed at all. They are best found on pelagic birding trips, including those from Half Moon Bay, Monterey, Ventura, and San Diego. They tend to be less common to the south. They are often found with blue whales, which also feed on krill.

Small alcid with thick, finch-like bill, much smaller than a football. All dark with white spot above eye; in flight shows pale belly. Adult has pale iris.

Pomarine Jaeger

Stercorarius pomarinus

L 17″ | **WS** 48″

All three species of jaegers migrate through California. The Pomarine Jaeger is the largest and bulkiest; in the breeding season, the thick bill has an orange base and the tail shows an odd blunt-tipped, spoon-shaped, central streamer. Like gulls, jaegers only slowly attain adulthood, passing through a series of immature plumages that can be difficult to identify. Pomarines tend to show the largest white wing patches. Pomarines are often the most frequently encountered jaeger on pelagic trips, seen harassing gulls in search of food. A few of these Arctic breeders winter in California waters; most continue their migration as far as South America.

Largest jaeger; breeding adult has long, spoon-like tail tips. Extensive dark cap, thick breast band.

Parasitic Jaeger

Stercorarius parasiticus

L 21" | **WS** 21"

This is the medium-size of the three jaegers (the less common and smaller Long-tailed Jaeger is not included in this guide). The Parasitic Jaeger plies its trade at coastal sites such as Monterey and Santa Cruz, relentlessy chasing terns and sometimes gulls in fast, incredibly maneuverable flight; the jaeger steals and eats the other birds' prey. Adults in breeding plumage have short, spiky tail streamers. Both the Parasitic and the Pomarine Jaeger also have a more rarely seen dark morph.

Breeding adult brownish above, white below, with dark cap. Central tail feathers pointed.

Breeding adult's spiky central tail feathers obvious in flight. Pale below with indistinct breast band.

Heermann's Gull

Larus heermanni

L 19.5″ | **WS** 43″

The dark, red-billed Heermann's Gull is one of the most strikingly patterned of all of the world's gulls; the head is white during the breeding season. Most Heermann's Gulls breed in Baja California, then migrate north to spend the off-season in California. Found year-round from Monterey Bay south, they arrive in northern California as early as July and return south by November. They are common on southern beaches, such as in Malibu and Santa Monica, but progressively less abundant to the north. In warm water years, more move north. A small population breeds on Roberts Lake in Monterey, a good place to see this species.

Breeding adult unique, dark gray with white head, red bill, and black legs.

First-year immature uniform chocolate brown with black legs, orange-pink bill base.

Bonaparte's Gull

Chroicocephalus philadelphia

L 13" | **WS** 30.5"

This highly migratory little gull, named for an ornithologist nephew of Napoleon, breeds in the boreal forest. Tern-like in size and shape, Bonaparte's Gulls do not dive, but rather hover over the water, picking food from the surface. Preferred feeding sites include aeration ponds at sewage treatment plants and other bodies of water with lots of floating food. Between mid-October and May, these gulls can be found along the coast and on reservoirs, inland lakes, and estuaries. Spring migration is mainly up the coast, often up to a few miles offshore. Palo Alto Baylands and the Salton Sea are good sites to find them.

A small gull. Breeding adult with black hood and small black bill. Pale gray above, white below with striking orange legs.

Small gray-backed gull with orange legs. Small pointed bill, head with black ear spot.

In flight, gray above with white triangle on outer wing.

Mew Gull

Larus canus

L 17″ | **WS** 43.5″

The Mew Gull is the "small big gull," tiny in comparison to its similarly plumaged white-headed relatives, such as the California Gull. Mew Gulls have an adorable look about them with a large head, small bill, and big black eye. Breeding in the forests of the far northwest, essentially all Mew Gulls winter along the Pacific Coast. Between November and April, you can see Mew Gulls anywhere along the California coast, even in moist fields and estuaries. They are most common at northern sites such as Arcata Bay; small numbers are found in the Central Valley. Usually silent; the voice is higher-pitched and more nasal than the similar calls of a Ring-billed Gull.

A small gull with very long wings, dark eyes, tiny unmarked yellow bill, yellow legs, and medium-gray back. Breeding plumage with unmarked white head.

First-year immature like Ring-billed but smaller, small-billed, and washed brownish; entirely dark tail in flight.

Ring-billed Gull

Larus delawarensis

L 19″ | **WS** 43.5″

This common interior-breeding gull winters throughout California. Many nonbreeding immatures remain in the state through the summer. Ring-billed Gulls are found in all sorts of habitats, including parking lots. They are absent from the coast in the Bay Area counties, apparently preferring to feed in the Bay itself. The streaking on the head of winter adults is neat and fine, not messy as in the other white-headed gulls. Calls are scratchier and higher-pitched than in larger gulls; they often throw the head high up over the back when giving a call.

Medium sized gull with pale gray back, yellow eyes and legs, and yellow bill with bold black ring.

First-year immature dark-eyed and pink-legged, with sharply bicolored, pink-based bill. Pale gray back contrasts with browner wing; tail whitish with blackish band.

Western Gull

Larus occidentalis

L 24″ | **WS** 52″

Big and bulky, with thick bills, Western Gulls are the darkest-backed gull seen in most of California. The adult's bill is bright banana-yellow all year round. Nearly all Western Gulls breed in California; southern California breeders are slightly darker-backed than those in the northern part of the state. This gull is not classically migratory, but young birds often wander northward. Look for Western Gulls in any coastal city, including San Francisco, Los Angeles, and San Diego, or on beaches, parking lots, and building roofs—essentially anywhere. They are quite scarce away from the coast. Frequent hybridization with Glaucous-winged Gulls creates birds with an intermediate appearance. Calls are higher-pitched than those of Glaucous-winged.

Big, bulky, pot-bellied gull. Head white throughout year, bill banana-yellow with red spot; legs pink. Back darker gray than in other large gulls.

First-year immature messy and brownish, with bulky bill thickest near tip. Face usually has dusky mask. Paler below, tail entirely dark in flight.

Second-year immature has gray back, white rump, and black tail. The wings are brownish as in the first-year immature, but body more whitish.

Yellow-footed Gull

Larus livens

L 27″ | **WS** 60″

Very similar and closely related to the Western Gull, the Yellow-footed differs in its bright yellow legs and, more subtly, its darker back and larger bill. Young birds mature faster than Western, acquiring a dark gray back in the first year instead of the second year. This species is found mainly in the Gulf of California, though good numbers are present from July to September (fewer year-round) at the Salton Sea, where it should be looked for in southeastern areas such as Red Hill and Obsidian Butte. Voice is lower-pitched and more nasal than in the Western Gull.

Adult like Western Gull but thicker bill, darker back, and yellow legs.

First-year immature like Western but becomes gray-backed in first winter; thicker bill with orange base to lower and upper mandible.

Herring Gull

Larus argentatus

L 24″ | **WS** 55.5″

The Herring Gull is one of North America's most widespread and common gulls. They move south from Alaskan breeding areas to spend late September to late April in California, where they are most common on the northern and central coasts and, to a lesser extent, in the Central Valley. The best way to find them is to look through a large concentration of Western and California Gulls for a pale-backed adult gull with gleaming yellow eyes and an aggressive expression.

Adult pale-backed with black wing tips. Bright yellow eye creates angry impression. Head streaked in non-breeding plumage. Pink legs.

Immature brown with pale blaze at bill base; bill becomes pinkish at base in first winter. Wing coverts coarsely patterned, tail dark with pale notches at edge.

Glaucous-winged Gull

Larus glaucescens

L 21.5" | **WS** 51.5"

The bulky and big-billed Glaucous-winged is the only gull in North America whose wing tips match the back, even in immature birds. Always paler than Western Gulls, although the two species hybridize, producing many individuals of intermediate appearance. Glaucous-winged Gulls breed from Alaska to Washington; they arrive in California by early September and leave in early May. They are common on the coast, especially in the north, and smaller numbers appear inland; look for them in Arcata, Half Moon Bay, and Monterey. The voice is lower and calls are slower than those of Western Gulls.

Large and bulky with thick-tipped bill. Adult with gray wing tips similar in color to the gray back. Head variably streaked in nonbreeding plumage. Eye dark, legs pink.

In flight, gray wing tips very similar in color to rest of wings. Dark eye, pink legs.

First-year immature evenly pale brown, wing tips similar in color to back. Thick-tipped bill entirely black.

California Gull

Larus californicus

L 20″ | **WS** 51″

The state bird of Utah, the California Gull is resident in California, where it can be found essentially anywhere, from lakes in the Sierra to offshore ocean waters. The largest breeding colonies are in Mono Lake and, since the 1980s, South San Francisco Bay. This adaptable gull flourishes on food provided by humans at landfills and in parking lots. Of the large gulls with a red bill spot, only the California has greenish or yellow legs.

A large gull with mid-gray back and long-winged look. Long, parallel-sided bill has red spot and dark spot; eye dark, legs yellowish. Nonbreeding bird with shawl of dark streaking on head and back of neck.

Mid-size, long-winged, with tubular bill. First-year immature brown with distinctly bicolored bill, pinkish legs. Dark tail in flight.

Least Tern

Sternula antillarum

L 8.5" | **WS** 20"

The Least Tern is local and relatively rare in California, where it is officially listed as endangered. This smallest of our terns is found in the state between mid-April and mid-September; there are breeding colonies in the San Francisco Bay Area in Alameda and at southern California sites including the Santa Clara River Mouth, McGrath State Beach, Huntington State Beach, and Mission Bay.

A tiny tern with pale gray upperparts and short yellow legs. Black cap contrasts with white forehead and yellow bill with dark tip.

Black Tern

Chlidonias niger

L 9.5″ | **WS** 23″

This small dark tern of the marshes dives for prey, but it also captures insects on the wing after large hatches. Black Terns occur in California from mid-April to mid-October, but as a breeding bird, this species has been declining in the state and is now largely gone from the San Joaquin Valley; nesting still takes place in the upper Sacramento Valley and the northeast, the numbers highest following very wet winters. Black Terns in the Sacramento Valley favor rice fields. Large numbers stage at Tule Lake and the Salton Sea during fall migration. The call is a rasping *kjeef*.

A small tern with black bill and legs. Attractive breeding plumage is black with white vent.

Small tern with fine black bill. Nonbreeding birds dark gray above, white below, with dark "helmet" and spur on breast sides.

Forster's Tern

Sterna forsteri

L 13.5″ | **WS** 31″

The Forster's is the most widespread of California's smaller terns, breeding in coastal estuaries and on ponds in the northeast. The Forster's is the only smaller tern expected in winter, when they are common at coastal sites, foraging on wetlands, ponds, salt evaporation ponds, and shallow tidal areas. A classic tern, the Forster's Tern dives from a height to capture fish and other small prey; these birds spend a good portion of their time resting and preening, usually on a sand bar or berm where they can watch for approaching danger. Fall flocks of Forster's Terns should be checked for the rarer Common Tern. In summer, gives a rasping *keearrrrr.*

Medium-size tern with long forked tail, wings with silvery flash in flight. Breeding bird has black cap, orange bill with black tip.

Immature and winter birds have shorter forked tail, blackish bill, and dull orange legs. Distinctive black mask.

Caspian Tern

Hydroprogne caspia

L 20" | **WS** 50"

The Caspian Tern is the largest tern in the world, as large as a mid-sized gull. The thick, obviously pointed red bill identifies it. A migrant and breeder in the state, arriving in March and leaving by October, this is a fish eater, hunting in both freshwater and marine habitats. Caspians congregate in fall migration anywhere they can find fish, including hyper-saline lakes such as the Salton Sea. Watch them hunting day smelt in Half Moon or Humboldt Bay. Their resemblance to a pterodactyl is only increased by their loud, harsh *ka-rraaaaagghhh* scream; young birds give a begging whistle.

Huge, gull-sized tern. Pale gray above, with large red bill and black legs. Flat-topped head, black cap.

Thick red bill, dark cap in breeding plumage. Dark underside to primaries.

Royal Tern

Thalasseus maximus

L 18.5″ | **WS** 51″

Widespread on the coasts of North and South America and Africa, in California the Royal Tern extends to Morro Bay but is essentially absent from the slightly cooler waters to the north. Unlike Caspian Terns, Royal Terns remain into winter. A great place to see them is the breeding colony at Bolsa Chica. Intermediate in size between the larger Caspian and smaller, thinner-billed Elegant Tern, Royal Terns can be confused with both. Royals lose their black forehead early in the season, often while still nesting. They give a raspy *keerraa*.

A large tern with thick orange bill, black legs, and shaggy crest. In flight, underwing shows restricted black. Black crown in breeding plumage.

Nonbreeding plumage, acquired early in summer, appears bald with large white forehead. Thick orange bill, pale gray upperparts.

Elegant Tern

Thalasseus elegans

L 16" | **WS** 42"

This is California's most common tern on the coast from late summer into fall. Elegant Terns breed only in California and Baja California; after breeding, they migrate north, sometimes reaching Oregon, then fly south to winter off Peru and Chile. This slender tern has a long, thin bill that droops over its entire length; the bill ranges from yellow (usually in young birds) to red with an orange tip. Bolsa Chica is a great place to see Elegant Terns in summer; in fall, they are common on Monterey Bay and Half Moon Bay, with a few on San Francisco Bay. The young follow their parents for months after leaving the nest, uttering a single-syllable *kreek* contrasting with the adult's stronger, double-syllabled *krrr-reeek*.

Mid-size tern. Long, thin, droopy bill is reddish orange with paler tip. Long and very shaggy crest, black cap in breeding plumage.

In flight, slimmer than Royal Tern, with longer bill. Restricted black on underwing, unlike Caspian Tern.

Black Skimmer

Rynchops niger

L 17.5" | **WS** 45"

There are only three species of skimmer in the world, and we can see one of them in California. Skimmers are the only birds with a lower mandible longer than the upper. Flying smoothly over the water on very long and narrow wings, a skimmer opens its bill wide, "cutting" the water with the knife-like lower mandible. When it encounters prey, it snaps the bill shut and grabs the morsel. The Black Skimmer is most easily found on coastal wetlands and ponds in the south; it is common in Bolsa Chica. In San Francisco Bay, small numbers have recently colonized the Radio Road Ponds in Redwood Shores. Usually quiet, but has a soft barking call.

Unique, with lower mandible longer than upper. Black and white plumage, orange and black bill; long wings.

Skims water. Very long-winged, black and white plumage. Nonbreeding bird with white at neck base.

Rock Pigeon

Columba livia

L 13" | **WS** 23"

The city pigeon may be the bird most easily recognized by non-birders. The typical plumage of wild birds is gray and black, but the domestic varieties of this introduced species show a bewildering array of plumage colors, rusty, white, patchy, or even blackish. All have bright reddish pink legs and a noticeably white mass (called a "cere") at the base of the bill. Unlike most birds, Rock Pigeons may breed year-round. In their native range, they are cliff dwellers, but in California, they happily nest and roost on buildings, bridges, and warehouses. They feed on the ground. The song is a series of deep, purring coos.

Gray body with darker head, black stripes on folded wing. Stocky but long-winged, with short pinkish legs, fleshy white at base of short bill.

Gregarious and familiar in urban areas. Extremely variable coloration after millennia of domestication.

Band-tailed Pigeon

Patagioenas fasciata

L 14.5" | **WS** 25"

Band-tails are huge pigeons, with sturdy bodies and long tails. If a flock happens to descend on your backyard feeder, they will really eat a lot. They breed in taller forest, where the nests are very difficult to spot. Though present somewhere in California, especially in mountain forests, at any time of year, Band-tailed Pigeons are migratory, moving to different parts of the state in different seasons. They commute moderate distances from the breeding areas to feed at backyard feeders, on recently plowed fields, or on acorn-covered lawns. This is one of few birds that eat the fragrant, oily nuts of introduced eucalyptus trees. The hooting call is deeper and more resonant than a city pigeon's coo.

A large pigeon with long tail. Lead-gray body with white band on nape, yellow bill with black tip, yellow legs. Gray tail darker at base.

White-winged Dove

Zenaida asiatica

L 11.5" | **WS** 20"

This desert dove is very eye-catching when seen well. White-winged Doves are most common in California's desert southeast, but wanderers occasionally reach the coast or even northern California. They usually travel as singles or in pairs rather than flocks. They are especially common near towns, where they visit backyard bird feeders, and in agricultural areas in the desert zone. The edge of the Salton Sea and the banks of the Colorado River in the Imperial Valley are good places to look; large numbers congregate at the Palo Verde Ecological Reserve. Their melancholic cooing, *Who cooks for you?* is a common sound in the desert.

Attractive dove with large white wing patch. Brownish gray, tail with big white tip, pale blue skin around red eye. Black line on face below ear.

Eurasian Collared-Dove

Streptopelia decaocto

L 11.5" | **WS** 14"

The most recent addition to California's breeding birds, this species escaped from captivity in the Bahamas, reached Florida, and then spread quickly in twenty years or so all the way to the Pacific. It is now common throughout the state, often more common than the native Mourning Dove. The Collared-Dove seems to displace the smaller Mourning Dove from such preferred habitats as suburbs and small agricultural towns. The three-noted hoot is owl-like, *hoo HOO cup*; it also gives an annoyed, nasal *pheewwww* in flight.

Thickset dove with sandy gray plumage. Head squarish, nape with black and white collar. Outer feathers of square tail with big white tips.

Mourning Dove

Zenaida macroura

L 11″ | **WS** 17.5″

At one time the most common dove in California, the Mourning Dove is now rivaled in abundance by the larger, bulkier Eurasian Collared-Dove. The Mourning Dove is always smaller and slimmer, with a long pointed tail. Common at backyard bird feeders, on brushy edge, and in suburban areas, this California resident breeds almost throughout the year. The nest is a precariously sited, poorly built platform of sticks. Pairs or singles are often seen flying fast low over the ground with whistling wings. The Mourning Dove's name comes from its sad-sounding voice, a cooing *e'WOOO cooo cooo cooo*.

Slim, sandy-brown dove with long pointed tail. Black spots on inner wing, narrow black stripe below ear. In flight, pointed tail with white tips.

Common Ground-Dove

Columbina passerina

L 6.5″ | **WS** 10.5″

This sparrow-size dove with a rotund body and short tail is restricted to far southern California, especially in the interior desert. It can be common at the Salton Sea, often foraging on the ground in villages or agricultural areas next to the sea. Often seen in pairs, it is sometimes found with the Inca Dove, which is slimmer and longer-tailed with a scaly look to the plumage. Both of these small doves show rusty wing patches in flight. The song of the Common Ground-Dove is a rhythmic series of repeated upslurred coos, given at a rate of one per second, *whoop, whoop, whoop....*

Tiny, sandy-brown dove. Short black stripes on wings and scapulars, male with pinkish wash on breast and iridescent nape.

Yellow-billed Cuckoo

Coccyzus americanus

L 11" | **WS** 16"

Officially listed as endangered in California, the Yellow-billed Cuckoo is declining as its habitat—tall, mature forests along creeks and rivers—is cut and degraded. Cuckoos hunt caterpillars in cottonwood forests with willow edges. Late migrants, they arrive in late May to breed, mainly the Central Valley. Look for it in the Kern River Preserve, as well as along the Sacramento or Colorado rivers. The Yellow-billed Cuckoo's odd vocalizations include a loud *kup-kup-kup-kup-Kowp Kopw* and dove-like cooing.

Slim and mid-size, with long rounded tail; brown above, white below. Face looks slightly masked, largely yellow bill with curved culmen. Big white spots on tail feathers. In flight, has chestnut patch on primaries.

Greater Roadrunner

Geococcyx californianus

L 21″ | **WS** 19.5″

There is no bird like the roadrunner, a large, inquisitive predator with an impressive and expressive crest and equally communicative long tail. Roadrunners seem to come out of nowhere, moving fast with an almost reptilian gait as they hunt lizards, snakes, or large insects. They are most common in southern desert areas, such as Palm Springs and Calipatria in the Imperial Valley, but also range north to arid areas such as Lower Mines Road in the San Francisco Bay area. The song of the Roadrunner is the saddest of any California bird, a slowing series of six or more mournful, descending coos.

Unique terrestrial cuckoo with strong legs and long, expressive tail. Brown and striped. Powerful bill on slightly crested head; when excited, reveals blue and red skin behind eye.

Barn Owl

Tyto alba

L 14″ | **WS** 44″

This well-named owl often roosts and breeds in old buildings, under bridges, or in barns; it also takes readily to nest boxes and sometimes perches in dense palms or cypress. If you don't know of a habitual roost, it can be hard to find during the day. Barn Owls have a heart-shaped face and are very pale, sometimes distinctly cinnamon on the underparts. These owls do well even in urban areas if there are open spaces for hunting rodents. They are a common, nonmigratory resident in California; some may move to areas of higher rodent concentrations in the winter. Listen for them at night: the flight call is a loud, harsh sound like the release of compressed air, *scheeeeeeeeaak*.

A pale owl with a heart-shaped face and dark eyes. Some are buffier below. Some, mainly females, are buffier below.

Great Horned Owl

Bubo virginianus

L 21.5" | **WS** 48.5"

A common resident throughout California wherever there are large trees near open areas for hunting, the Great Horned is the classic owl, in plumage and in voice. It sports a cat-like face with huge yellow eyes and long feather "ears." The white throat patch is most obvious on calling birds. Great Horned Owls breed in nests built by hawks or other large birds. When roosting in the day, they usually remain hidden. Sometimes during daylight hours, these owls may perch in isolated trees, such as those along the road to the Tule Lake Visitors Center. The fluffy young perch near the nest, sometimes allowing close approach. At night, listen for *huu HOO hooo hoooo*; the male's voice is deeper than the female's.

A large owl with yellow eyes and long ear tufts. Cat-like face, noticeable white patch on throat. Very large, long talons.

Western Screech-Owl

Megascops kennicottii

L 9″ | **WS** 23″

This owl of open woodland and oak forest is a backyard bird in many suburban areas, but as common and as widespread as it is, it can be difficult to find, roosting deep within tree cavities or huddling, well-camouflaged by a tree trunk. Screech-owls will breed in nest boxes. They look like a miniature Great Horned Owl, but their small size, hardly larger than the palm of your hand, separates them easily. At night, listen for a series of perky hoots that become more closely spaced as the song goes on, *puup…puup…puup…puupuupuup*. The female utters a two-part rolling trill.

A small owl, gray and narrowly striped. Big yellow eyes and small ear tufts.

Northern Pygmy-Owl

Glaucidium gnoma

L 6.5″ | **WS** 13″

A tiny owl of dense coniferous forests. Unlike screech-owls, pygmy-owls have small heads and eyes, no "ear" tufts, and long tails. They will eat insects, but prefer small birds. They are most active at dawn and dusk, but are also seen out and about in the daylight, when their preference for perching high in tall trees can make them difficult to find. Listen for the commotion of small birds mobbing an owl. Uncommon in California, Northern Pygmy-Owls are found in coastal mountains, the Transverse Mountains, and the Sierra. In the San Francisco Bay area, they can be found on Gazos Creek along the coast or in the higher reaches of Del Puerto Canyon. They can also be seen on Empire Grade Road in the south. The unassuming voice is a slow series of piping hoots.

A tiny, small-headed owl with long, narrow tail. Warm brown, with pale spots on forehead, dark breast, and striped belly; yellow eyes, boldly banded tail.

Burrowing Owl

Athene cunicularia

L 8.5" | **WS** 21.5"

This unusual and well-named owl really does like to go underground, roosting and breeding in burrows taken over from squirrels and other mammals. This small owl is commonly seen perching on the ground or poking only its head out of its burrow. Fence posts and hay bales are also favored perches. Though found almost throughout the state, absent only from the forested northwest, the coastal mountains, and the Sierra, the Burrowing Owl is a species of conservation concern in California, as the open habitats it requires have decreased markedly, particularly in the San Francisco Bay area. They are still common in the Imperial Valley, on the Carrizo Plain, and in parts of the Central Valley. Resident numbers are augmented by migrants in winter. Typically silent during the day.

Terrestrial and diurnal. A pale brown owl with darker breast and white eyebrows over yellow eyes. Long, white-feathered legs.

Short-eared Owl

Asio flammeus

L 15" | **WS** 37"

This mid-sized owl with very long wings can be seen at dawn or dusk flying over the fields like an oversized moth. Short-eared Owls flap their wings slowly and mechanically, and often glide or even soar. Barn Owls, which share their open-country habitat, are more strictly nocturnal. Resident in the northern part of the state, migrants occur in central California; they are rare or absent in the south. Good places to look for them include the Klamath Basin, Panoche Valley, and Carrizo Plain. Between October and March, they can also be seen in the Bay area on Wavecrest Road in Half Moon Bay or in Coyote Hills. Usually silent.

Flies over grasslands. Warm brown, paler below and streaked. Small ear tufts often not visible. Small yellow eyes surrounded by black "mascara."

Often flies in daylight. Warm buffy patch on upper side of primaries, underwing pale with dark "comma" at "wrist." Underparts darkest on densely streaked breast.

Spotted Owl

Strix occidentalis

L 18.5" | **WS** 40"

Dependent on old, tall forest, this owl has played a prominent role in California's environmental history. The northern population listing as threatened under the Endangered Species Act changed forestry practices across the Pacific Northwest. The Spotted Owl is resident in California's coastal mountains and the Sierra, but essentially absent between the Golden Gate and the mountains in Monterey County. Look for it at Muir Woods in Marin or in Calaveras Big Trees State Park in the Sierra. Dark like wet bark, this owl hides well, and may roost near people without being detected. Spotted Owls become active before nightfall. The hoot is a four-parted *huup hoo hoo, hooo.*

Mid-size dark owl of forest. Dark eyes on dark face, whitish spots on belly.

Northern Saw-whet Owl

Aegolius acadicus

L 7.5″ | **WS** 17.5″

This large-headed little owl is more boldly patterned than screech- and pygmy-owls, with a white face and thickly striped underparts. It lacks ear tufts. Saw-whets are found in tall coniferous forests throughout California's mounts; they are absent from the Central Valley and desert. They eat insects and small rodents. The best way to see this species is on an outing specifically for owls. Big Basin State Park in Santa Cruz and Butano State Park in San Mateo are good places; they are also found in the San Gabriel Mountains. The call is a quick series of piping hoots, about two per second, much faster than the pygmy-owl.

Cute small owl with large head, yellow eyes, and white eyebrows. Brown above with white spots, whitish below with broad mocha-colored streaks.

Lesser Nighthawk

Chordeiles acutipennis

L 8.4" | **WS** 21.5"

Our two nighthawks can be difficult to distinguish: the Lesser has slightly rounder wings and a pale wing band closer to the wing tip than on the Common. Lesser also occurs in more arid areas. The male's wing band is white, the female's buffy. Lesser Nighthawks breed mainly in the south and the desert, with some in the southern Central Valley. Nighthawks become active in the evening, but sometimes they can be seen in the middle of the day. Numbers can be seen at the Palo Verde Ecological Preserve; also look for it in Death Valley and the Imperial Valley. The voice is an odd, insect-like rolling trill.

Pointed wings, long notched tail. Wing patch, white in male, buffy in female, about half way out on primaries. Inner primaries and secondaries strongly spotted golden.

Common Nighthawk

Chordeiles minor

L 9″ | **WS** 21.5″

This highly migratory nighthawk winters in South America. Like the Lesser, it flies with deep, erratic wing beats. Very rare on the coast, Common Nighthawks are found east of the Sierra and in the northeast part of the state. In August, good numbers occur over Bridgeport Reservoir and in the Mono Lake area. The voice is an odd nasal *peent* given in flight; in display, the male makes a loud swooshing *hoooov* as it dives through the air.

Often roosts parallel to branch; marbled above, barred below, male with white throat.

Pointed wings, long notched tail. White wing patch of male close to base of primaries; female's white wing patch is narrower. No golden spotting on inner primaries.

Common Poorwill

Phalaenoptilus nuttallii

L 8" | **WS** 17"

Large-headed and short-tailed, the Common Poorwill is usually found by its distinctive *poor-wheeuup* call. It is widespread in California, but local in the north and absent from moister areas. Much more commonly heard than seen, poorwills can be looked for on the edge of open conifer and oak woodlands and in the higher, shrubbier areas of deserts. Flushed, they fly away on rounded wings; the male has white tail corners. At least some are migratory, and poorwills can be found out of habitat on the southward migration in September and October. They remain through winter in the southern part of the state, entering torpor in cold weather: the bird's metabolic rate slows to conserve energy.

Nocturnal. A small, big-headed nightjar with a short tail. Male with white throat and tail corners.

Black Swift

Cypseloides niger

L 7″ | **WS** 15″

A much sought-after species, this uncommon to rare swift breeds in in scattered populations in the Sierra, in the San Jacinto and San Bernardino Mountains, and on the central coast of San Mateo and Santa Cruz Counties. The nests are placed on the walls of sea caves and behind waterfalls, such as in McArthur Burney Falls Memorial Park northeast of Redding. New tracking technology has recently revealed that Black Swifts winter along the Amazon. During spring migration in May, Black Swifts are more widespread in California, particularly in the northwest. A record count of 650 was made in McKinleyville a few years ago. Usually silent.

A large blackish swift with a large head and long notched tail.

Black Swifts make moss and twig nests on rock ledges near water.

Vaux's Swift

Chaetura vauxi

L 4.5″ | **WS** 11″

This small dark swift arrives in April and stays until mid-October, nesting in old trees with rotten middles in northern California, the Sierra, and the forests of the northeast. There are also populations in Marin, the Santa Cruz Mountains, and Big Sur. The semicircular nest is pasted to the inside of the hollow tree with saliva. In the rest of the state, this is a migrant, thousands often roosting in large chimneys in the fall. Traditional sites are in downtown Los Angeles and at the McNear Brickyard in San Rafael.

A small brownish swift with short tail, paler rump and throat.

White-throated Swift

Aeronautes saxatalis

L 6.5″ | **WS** 13.5″

At all seasons, this is the most common and most easily encountered swift in most of California, absent only from the moister northwest. The bold black and white pattern and slim, long-tailed shape make this the most striking of our swifts. Originally nesting in cliffside crevices, White-throated Swifts now also breed in buildings and in the drainage holes of freeway overpasses The voice is a long series of increasingly scratchy notes spiraling downward in pitch. The downward slide may recall a Canyon Wren, but the swift's notes are much scratchier.

A slim, long-tailed black and white swift. Has white throat, mid-belly, and flank patches.

Anna's Hummingbird

Calypte anna

L 4" | **WS** 4.5"

This tiny bird is California's common year-round backyard hummingbird. Adaptable and hardy, Anna's Hummingbirds are resident throughout their range; they can handle even freezing nights, presumably entering a type of torpor. They are territorial at feeders, driving other hummingbirds away. Fewer adult males are seen than females and immature birds. The male's aerial dive ends with a sharp noise caused by the vibrating tail feathers; its songs are twittering and pleasant. Anna's Hummingbirds begin nesting during the winter rainy period, when flowers start to bloom.

A sturdy, rather pot-bellied hummingbird. Male has raspberry throat feathers (gorget) that extend onto crown and onto the side of the head as whiskers. Belly gray with green flanks.

Female with mid-length bill, green above and gray below with greener flanks; often a raspberry patch in the center of the throat. Stocky and thickset.

Costa's Hummingbird

Calypte costae

L 3.5" | **WS** 4.5"

Found in arid areas, this bird is the smaller and slimmer relative of the Anna's Hummingbird. The male's throat feathers (gorget) are purple instead of raspberry, and the female is much whiter below than the female Anna's. Closely associated with desert environments, the Costa's is easy to see in the Palm Springs area, where it is a backyard bird. Much less common in central California, but Del Puerto Canyon Road is a good place to see them. This species is resident in the south and the deserts, but only a summer visitor farther north. The song of the male is a very high-pitched buzz that rises and then falls.

Small hummingbird. Male with violet gorget that extends to crown and long whiskers on sides of neck. Green back and flanks. Smaller than Anna's.

Female small with mid-size bill, green above and whitish below. Like Anna's but smaller and more whitish below.

Rufous Hummingbird

Selasphorus rufus

L 3″ | **WS** 4″

Except for adult males, the Rufous and Allen's Hummingbirds are exceedingly difficult or even impossible to distinguish. The two are also similar ecologically, but the Rufous is the more northerly breeder, nesting as far north as Alaska. In California, the Rufous is a migrant, peaking in March and heading south later than the Allen's. In central and northern California after August, a hummingbird in the genus *Selasphorus* is almost surely a Rufous. The southbound migration passes mostly through the Sierra, while spring migrants occur closer to the coast.

Male rufous on back, flanks, tail and face. Small, with pointed tail and reddish gorget.

Female nearly identical to female Allen's. Note triangle of iridescent orange feathers at the base of throat.

Allen's Hummingbird

Selasphorus sasin

L 3.5″ | **WS** 4.5″

This is largely a bird of the coastal slope, absent from the interior. The Allen's Hummingbird has two different populations in California. The migrant population arrives in the north and central part of the state in late winter and leaves again in mid-summer; the sedentary population, originally resident on the Channel Islands and Palos Verdes Peninsula, is now found in continental southern California. The voice is nearly identical to that of the Rufous Hummingbird, but higher-pitched and sharper than the Anna's Hummingbird's.

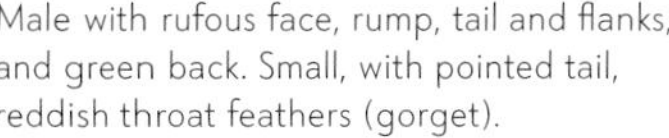

Male with rufous face, rump, tail and flanks, and green back. Small, with pointed tail, reddish throat feathers (gorget).

Female green above with cinnamon flanks and base of tail. Not safely separable in the field from female Rufous.

Calliope Hummingbird

Selasphorus calliope

L 3.25" | **WS** 4.25"

North America's lightest bird—about the weight of a penny—resembles a tubby bumblebee in flight. The male is the only hummingbird with striped throat feathers (gorget). All ages and both sexes have a distinctive facial appearance with a small white notch in front of the bill. Breeding in the Sierra, the Calliope Hummingbird is a migrant in the rest of California. It arrives in March; adult males leave for the south by mid-July, while females and young remain into August. Quiet, but males give a very thin descending whistle.

Tiny. Male with raspberry-striped throat feathers (gorget), white spot between eye and bill. Green above, whitish below.

Female green above with buffy belly, distinctive white notch above bill base.

Black-chinned Hummingbird

Archilochus alexandri

L 3.5" | **WS** 4.25"

The Black-chinned is a very long-billed hummingbird of riverside vegetation and the edges of oak woodland. Both sexes have a dull brownish tint to the upperparts. The male's throat feathers (gorget) is black with a purple band at the lower edge; females are smaller and paler below than female Anna's, with a proportionately longer bill and slimmer profile. Black-chinned Hummingbirds migrate or breed species over much of California, but are rarer in the moist northwest. They are uncommon in the San Francisco Bay area, found in the East Bay, with a few in the Alviso area of the South Bay; much more common farther south and east. Gives a sharp chase call.

Small hummingbird with long bill. Greenish above with brown wash, brownish green flanks. White spot behind eye, throat feathers (gorget) blackish with purplish blue border.

Female dull greenish above, whitish below with darker flanks. Dusky mask and white spot behind eye.

Belted Kingfisher

Megaceryle alcyon

L 12.5" | **WS** 21"

North America's most widespread kingfisher is the only member of its family in California. The large head and shaggy crest, blue upperparts, and plunge-diving behavior easily identify this bird. Belted Kingfishers are widespread residents throughout the state, less frequent in desert areas. They are found on rivers, lakes, ponds, and even ocean harbors, where they fish from a low perch. The highest numbers are found in the moist northwest. They build their nests in burrows dug into a dirt bank; the numbers of this common but not abundant bird are probably limited by the availability of such sites. The male's breast band is blue, while the female has both a blue and a rusty band. Kingfishers give a loud chattering rattle, often in flight.

Big shaggy head, thick dagger-like bill. Blue upperparts, head, and breast band. White neck and underparts, female with rusty lower breast band. Very short tail.

Lewis's Woodpecker

Melanerpes lewis

L 10.5″ | **WS** 20″

The Lewis's Woodpecker prefers savanna habitats with large, often dead trees. The flapping flight of the Lewis's Woodpecker is not undulating but steady, almost like a crow's. They fly out from a perch to take flying insects, but in winter switch to acorns. Found over a large part of the state, absent from the wet northwest and the central coast, some California populations of this species are permanent residents; in other areas, migrants and wintering birds are seen during the non-breeding season. Call is a nasal *kjeeff*.

Gorgeous, with pinkish red belly, red face, and greenish glossed blackish upperparts. Also has gray neck band dividing black of head from back.

Williamson's Sapsucker

Sphyrapicus thyroideus

L 9" | **WS** 15.5"

The male and female of this beautiful and uncommon woodpecker look very different from each other. Neither sex looks very much like the other sapsuckers, though they do have a white rump and, in the male, a large white wing patch. Like other sapsuckers, this species drills holes in living trees and harvests the sweet liquid. Williamson's Sapsucker breeds at low densities in high-elevation lodgepole pine forest in the Sierra, moving up and down in elevation with the seasons. Look for it in the Bear Valley Ski Area in the Sierra or at Bluff Lake in the San Bernardino Mountains. Call is a loud *queeahhh*; tree-drumming starts fast, then slows.

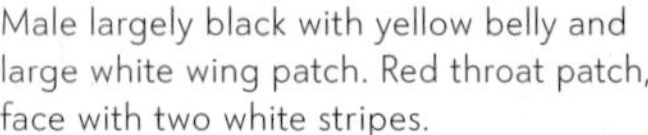

Male largely black with yellow belly and large white wing patch. Red throat patch, face with two white stripes.

Female barred throughout with darker breast and pale yellow belly. Head brownis with two indistinct pale stripes on face.

Red-breasted Sapsucker

Sphyrapicus ruber

L 8″ | **WS** 15″

Common in forested areas of the north, the Sierra, and mountains in the south, this sapsucker is particularly fond of conifer forests with cottonwoods, alders, or other softwood deciduous trees, into which they drill neat rows of shallow holes to incite the flow of sap. The sapsuckers drink the sap and eat the insects it draws; early in the season, hummingbirds visit these sapsucker "wells" too. These quiet, sneaky woodpeckers are resident in the state, most common in the moist northwest; migrants from the north winter on the central coast. Northern birds have more extensive red on the head. The call is a nasal *njeeeahhh* that drops towards the end.

Sexes alike. Largely red head and throat with white stripe on face at base of bill. Black above with white wing patch and white lines on back; paler underparts.

Ladder-backed Woodpecker

Picoides scalaris

L 6.5" | **WS** 13"

This small woodpecker is a common bird of desert scrub, riparian thickets, mesquite woods, and towns in the desert southeast. The Ladder-backed has buffy underparts and more white in the plumage and face than the Nuttall's Woodpecker; the Ladder-backed's face shows an open black triangle with a white center. Look for this species at the Salton Sea and in Palm Springs. The *pik* call is very similar to the Downy Woodpecker's, but lower-pitched; the rattle call ends with harsher notes than the Downy's.

Barred black and white above to nape, with more white than black. Complex face pattern; red hind-crown in male. Breast sides streaked, white underparts with smoky wash.

Nuttall's Woodpecker

Picoides nuttallii

L 6.5" | **WS** 13"

This resident California specialty is restricted to oak and other open woodlands in our state and small portions of Oregon and Baja California; it is absent from the far northwest and east of the Cascades and Sierra. Common in suburban areas, it is usually seen singly or in pairs. The black and white "laddered" back separates it from the Hairy and Downy; it is much darker on the face than the Ladder-backed Woodpecker, a desert bird seldom found with the Nuttall's. Only the male has red on the nape. Gives a two-note *pit-tik* call; the slow, rasping rattle recalls that of a Belted Kingfisher.

Barred black and white above, with more black than white and unbarred black band on nape. Complex face pattern darker than Ladder-backed, pure white below with spotted breast sides and flanks. Red hind-crown in male.

Downy Woodpecker

Picoides pubescens

L 6″ | **WS** 11″

Downy and Hairy Woodpeckers are both distinguished from the Nuttall's Woodpecker by the white stripe down the back. The Downy is smaller than the Hairy and relatively smaller billed; the black bars on the Downy's outer tail feathers are a key feature when visible. The Downy feeds on smaller lateral branches than the Hairy and is more acrobatic, almost hanging from the branch to reach its prey. Downy Woodpeckers are widespread residents everywhere but the desert, often common in backyards. The call is weaker than that of the Hairy, a sharp *pik* without conspicuous emphasis; the descending rattle has a squeaky quality. Their tree-drumming is slow and brief.

Small black and white woodpecker with short bill. White stripe on back, white stripes on face, outer tail white with black bars. Female lacks red on hind crown.

Hairy Woodpecker

Picoides villosus

L 8.5″ | **WS** 14.5″

The Hairy Woodpecker is very similar to the smaller Downy Woodpecker; the Hairy's white outer tail feathers are unspotted. Hairy Woodpeckers are common residents in California anywhere there is forest, even in wooded suburbs; they are less likely to visit backyards than the Downy. They are most common in the coastal mountains of the north and central parts of the state, and absent from the desert southeast. The *PEEK* note is more strident and louder than that of the Downy, while the rattle call is more forceful and does not fall in pitch. The drumming is quite different from the Downy's, each bout fast and long.

Medium-size black and white woodpecker with long bill. White stripe on back, white stripes on face, unbarred white outer tail feathers. Male with red on hind crown.

White-headed Woodpecker

Picoides albolarvatus

L 8.5″ | **WS** 17″

This uncommon bird is a truly western woodpecker, much sought-after by birders for its elegant appearance. Resident in the Sierra, the southern mountain ranges, and the coastal mountains of the far north, the White-headed Woodpecker is particularly fond of open and old ponderosa pine forests, where it feeds by flaking off bark in search of insects, often low on the trunks. Look for it in Calaveras Big Trees State Park and Sequoia National Forest. The calls include a sharp double note *pit-tik* and a long rattle; the drum is medium-fast and long.

Distinctive appearance: entirely black to nape with contrasting white head and wing patch, visible when perched. Male has red on hind crown.

Acorn Woodpecker

Melanerpes formicivorus

L 8.5" | **WS** 15"

Truly dependent on acorns and the bugs that eat acorns, the Acorn Woodpecker is always found in oak woodlands in the Central Valley, on the central and southern coastal lowlands. Groups of woodpeckers cooperate to collect acorns in the fall, which they then store in "granaries," dead trees or wooden power-line poles with acorn-sized holes drilled into them; the acorns feed the birds through the winter. Such cooperation takes place even in the breeding season, when many birds—typically sets of brothers—do not nest themselves but instead help others raise young. A black band between the white forehead and the red crown identifies the female. Vocal, giving a nasal *WEK-ah WEK-ah WEK-ah*.

Clown-faced. Red cap and white forehead contrast with black around bill and rest of face. Black above with white wing patches, white below with black breast and streaks.

Northern Flicker

Colaptes auratus

L 11.5" | **WS** 18"

The warm buffy and brown coloration, flash of red, black crescent on the breast, and large, perfectly round spots on the belly make this a fantastic-looking bird. The adaptable Northern Flicker is the largest woodpecker commonly encountered in California, found in open areas with some larger trees, edge habitats, and even suburban backyards. They sometimes land on the ground to feed or to "ant," picking up angry ants and placing them on their feathers to kill parasites. Found throughout the state except in the desert, where the similar Gilded Flicker takes over. The Yellow-shafted race visits in winter, identify it by yellow underwings, red crescent on nape, and a black (not red) moustache on males. Calls include a loud *keew* and a loud series *wiik wiik wiik wiik wiik*....

A large, colorful woodpecker. Gray head with brown crown, upperparts sandy brown with black bars, creamy white below with black chest and round black spots. Underwings and undertail salmon red. Male has red moustache.

Female like male but lacks red moustache. Salmon red of wings and tail often invisible when perched.

Pileated Woodpecker

Dryocopus pileatus

L 17.5" | **WS** 27.5"

Our largest woodpecker, and the only one with a crest, this huge species is not frequently encountered except in the far northeast, where it is resident at low densities in conifer forests, the coastal mountains south to Santa Cruz County, and the Sierra. It seems to be increasing on the central coast. Look for the large and rectangular excavations Pileated makes while foraging on dead or dying limbs. More often heard than seen; the loud *week week week week*... has a more laughing and cackling quality than the similar call of the Northern Flicker.

Huge woodpecker with pointed red crest. Black and white, with striped face, long pointed black tail, white patch at base of primaries, much white on underwing in flight. Red whisker on male.

American Kestrel

Falco sparverius

L 10.5" | **WS** 22"

The most colorful of our falcons, with notable plumage differences between the sexes, American Kestrels hunt voles and large insects in open areas. Their typical hunting style is to hover over their unsuspecting prey, flying in one spot on rapidly beating wings; when the time is right, they drop and grasp the rodent with their talons. Kestrels breed in cavities, often in a large snag, but they also use nest boxes. They are resident throughout California, with migrants from the north arriving in winter, when large numbers congregate in the Imperial Valley, Panoche Valley, and Central Valley. They are quite vocal, emitting an alarmed *killy killy killy killy*....

Slim, colorful falcon with two black bars on face. Male has blue-gray wings, rusty body with dark bars, and rusty tail with black band near tip.

Female is barred on back and tail, off-white below with rusty streaks. Gray cap and two dark bars on face.

Graceful almost effortless flyer; hovers when scanning for prey. Note strong black band on male's tail, weaker on female's.

Merlin

Falco columbarius

L 10.5″ | **WS** 47.5″

Slightly larger, stockier, and shorter-tailed than kestrels, Merlins are small but aggressive falcons, often appearing out of nowhere and causing a commotion among smaller birds, then leaving as quickly as they arrived. They chase their prey down in midair or pounce after a sneak attack. Merlins breed in the boreal forest, wintering in California from mid-September to early May. Merlins seem to be found anywhere small birds are found, on forest edges and mudflats, in open country and suburbia. On the southbound migration, peaking in mid-October, they are easily seen at Hawk Hill in Marin. Usually silent in the non-breeding season.

Small, stocky, dark falcon with a weak face pattern. Adult male blue-toned above, marked with cinnamon-brown below.

Pointed wings and strongly banded tail. Females and immatures brown above, streaked brown below.

Peregrine Falcon

Falco peregrinus

L 16.5" | **WS** 41"

This is the speed demon among the falcons, diving on its prey in an incredibly fast stoop. Peregrines knock smaller birds unconscious by hitting them at high speed with their body and closed talons. At other times, they fly in fast and low, keeping out of sight until they pounce on their prey before it can react. Peregrines are especially fond of shorebirds, making any mudflat with migrants a good place to watch for them. In urban areas, where they breed on buildings and under bridges, they feed mainly on pigeons. Peregrines are found year-round throughout California, but migrants also pass through the state; Arctic Peregrines have a paler plumage and a narrower "moustache." The voice is a cackling *yaak yaak yaak*....

Large, muscular, and bulky falcon with dark helmet and broad "moustache." Adult blue-gray above, pale and variably barred below, buffy wash on breast. At rest, flight feathers (primaries) reach to tail tip.

Immature brownish above, streaked below with white tail tip.

Prairie Falcon

Falco mexicanus

L 16.5″ | **WS** 40″

Though our two large falcons are sometimes found together, the Prairie Falcon prefers more open, arid habitats than the Peregrine, including desert. In the breeding season, Prairie Falcons are found east of the Sierra; Mono Lake is a good place to look for them in the desert. From October to March, birds from the rest of the breeding range can be found in the Panoche Valley, Klamath Basin, and Central Valley grasslands. Unlike Peregrines, the Prairie Falcon takes many ground squirrels and other small mammals, pouncing on them in a sneak attack. The hardy Prairie Falcon winters even in snowbound areas such as the Klamath Basin and Tule Lake.

A large, pale falcon, sandy brown above with noticeable but narrow "moustache." Whitish below, streaked or barred. Wings stop well short of tail tip.

Pointed wings and long tail, pale plumage with unique dark patch on underwing.

Olive-sided Flycatcher

Contopus cooperi

L 7.5" | **WS** 13"

The Olive-sided Flycatcher is widespread, although declining, in mountain conifers from the Oregon border to the Sierra, Coastal Mountains, and San Diego County. Olive-sided Flycatchers like forest edge and openings rather than closed woodland. They arrive on their California breeding grounds in mid-April and leave by late September. Similar to the closely related Western Wood-Pewee, but stockier, larger-billed, and shorter-tailed, they inhabit taller trees and forage from a dead branch higher up in the canopy. They typically return to the same high branch after flying out to catch bees, wasps, and other insects. The song is a loud, easily remembered *quick, free-beer!*

Stocky flycatcher with very long wings and stout bill. Dusky breast and flanks outline a white central belly. Hidden white patch on sides of rump sometimes shows.

Western Wood-Pewee

Contopus sordidulus

L 5.75″ | **WS** 10″

A common breeding visitor of open forests and forest edge, found throughout the state except in the Central Valley. Western Wood-Pewees start to arrive in mid-April and stay to mid-October, when they leave for the wintering grounds on the edge of the Amazon basin. In typical pewee style, they fly out to catch an insect and return to the same perch. Unlike the Olive-sided, pewees tend to feed in the forest mid-story, not high in the canopy. The subtly marked olive-green plumage resembles that of the smaller *Empidonax* flycatchers, but pewees have very long wings with dull wing bars, a plain face, and short legs. Learn the voice, and you will hear pewees everywhere, a rough-sounding *feeeeuuurrrr* that usually descends in pitch.

Slim flycatcher with tiny legs and very long wings. Dusky overall, no eye ring, dull wing bars. Paler below, with dusky breast; flanks paler than in Olive-sided.

Willow Flycatcher

Empidonax traillii

L 6″ | **WS** 8.5″

The Willow Flycatcher is a local breeder in California, with distinct populations in the far northwest and the south. That population, the Southwestern Willow Flycatcher, is endangered due to habitat loss; its stronghold is Camp Pendleton, where it breeds in riparian thickets. Much more common and widespread in migration, numbers can be found at such desert sites as Butterbredt Spring and Galileo Hill. California breeders arrive late in spring, usually in mid-May, and remain into late September; peak fall migration is in August. Listen for a buzzy *fitz-wurr*, with the second note harsher than the first; the call is a dry *whit*.

Brownish flycatcher with dark face and nearly no eye ring. Paler below, dull indistinct wing bars; resembles wood-pewee but paler below, with shorter wings.

Gray Flycatcher

Empidonax wrightii

L 5.75″ | **WS** 8.75″

A flycatcher of arid and shrubby habitats, especially sagebrush, the Gray Flycatcher is found east of the Sierra and, in smaller numbers, in the far south. Breeding birds arrive in April and leave by the end of September. Some also migrate on the coastal slope, mainly in the south. The shrubby dry habitat, washed-out look, and noticeable tail-pumping identify this species. It is more grayish than the Dusky, with a longer, black-tipped bill. The call note is a dry *whit,* like the Dusky's. The song is made up of two phrases, often alternated: a harsh *jirriip* and a mellower *tidoo*.

Slim, long-tailed, pale grayish flycatcher. Long narrow bill with dark tip to orange mandible. White eye ring indistinct on pale face, habitually dips tail.

Dusky Flycatcher

Empidonax oberholseri

L 5.5″ | **WS** 8.5″

A mountain species, though absent from the moister Coastal Ranges, the Dusky Flycatcher breeds in shrubby thickets in deciduous forest openings, choosing more open sites than the dense conifers preferred by the very similar Hammond's Flycatcher. Dusky Flycatchers arrive in April; most are gone by October. They have a shorter wing and relatively longer tail than the Hammond's. Dusky's *whit* call is very unlike the peeping note of the Hammond's. The song is three-parted, a high *sibip* followed by a rough *guerrrpp* and a high *suweep*.

Olive-gray flycatcher with long tail; darker bill than Gray Flycatcher. Similar to Hammond's, but shorter wing tip, longer tail, longer bill.

Hammond's Flycatcher

Empidonax hammondii

L 5″ | **WS** 8.75″

A flycatcher of coniferous forest, where it often stays high in the trees. The Hammond's breeds in the northern mountains and halfway down the Sierra; as a migrant, it is most common in the south. Hammond's Flycatchers arrive in April, and some remain into October, lingering later than most Dusky Flycatchers. The large head, small bill, and eye ring is similar to Ruby-crowned Kinglet. In fall, this species can be more boldly plumaged, with a yellow belly and distinctly green back contrasting with the gray head. The call is a *piip,* unlike that of any other *Empidonax* flycatcher. The song is made up of three two-syllable phrases, the middle phrase scratchy and the last one rough and low: *tsi-pik, svrrrk, Grrr-vik.*

Olive flycatcher with tiny bill, short tail. Similar to Dusky, but longer wing tip, more contrasting grayish head, and bolder eye ring.

Pacific-slope Flycatcher

Empidonax difficilis

L 6" | **WS** 8.5"

California's most widespread and common "empid" (*Empidonax* flycatcher) keeps to low or mid-levels in dark coniferous or mixed forest, often near water. It is absent from the desert and the Central Valley as a breeder, but can be seen there during migration. This species arrives as early as late March and remains into October. This is the most yellowish of our empids; the eye ring has a tear-drop-like point at the rear. The head can look slightly peaked; nervously twitches the tail upwards. The male gives an up-slurred contact note *psuweep!* The high-pitched song is a three-parted *pitsee, ptk, seee*. The Channel Islands population has a slightly different voice.

Green flycatcher, washed yellow below. Often looks to have a peaked head, mandible (bill) unmarked bright orange. Eye ring comes to a point behind eye.

Black Phoebe

Sayornis nigricans

L 6.25″ | **WS** 11″

Resident over much of California, with individuals from elsewhere arriving to winter, the Black Phoebe shows a clear predilection for water, especially when breeding. Although not numerous, they perch conspicuously in the open in suburban areas; this is perhaps the flycatcher most likely to be seen in a backyard. Black Phoebes commonly nest on bridges and other structures. They sing through much of the year, a monotonous sequence of two rising and falling notes, *pichrrr pitchuu pitchrrr pitchuu....* The call a slurred *tweew.*

Blackish with white belly; constantly dips tail.

Say's Phoebe

Sayornis saya

L 6.75″ | **WS** 13″

More likely to be found in open and arid country than the Black Phoebe, the hardy, cold-resistant Say's Phoebe is particularly fond of flat to rolling short grassland, pastures, and ranch houses. It is a widespread breeder in the interior and south, but is seen in the northwest only as a migrant; some winter on the coast. Numbers increase with the arrival of northern birds in winter, when populations can be high in the Imperial Valley or on the Carrizo Plain. This colorful flycatcher's tawny underparts may recall a Western Kingbird, which is far more unusual in winter than the phoebe. The Say's perches on a stalk or fencepost, seldom more than six feet off the ground. In the nonbreeding season, it gives a mellow, muffled *pheeeww*.

Warm gray flycatcher with darker mask and contrasting blackish tail. Pumpkin-colored belly and vent. Often flares tail.

Ash-throated Flycatcher

Myiarchus cinerascens

L 8″ | **WS** 12″

The "British Bobby" whistle call *kibrrrrr!* is often heard in oak woodland and thick chaparall, but this elongated flycatcher can be shy and difficult to see. Ash-throated Flycatchers return from their Mexican wintering grounds as early as late March in the south; most are gone by August, with some lingering into October. They breed throughout the state, but are patchily distributed in the desert and distinctly more rare on the coastal slope north of Eureka. The larger, larger-billed Brown-crested Flycatcher is found in the Imperial Valley and locally elsewhere in the desert southeast. Its voice is more raucous than that of the Ash-throated, which sings a pleasant repeated *kibrriik, kee-brrbrr....*

A slim, long-tailed flycatcher with a puffy crest and moderate-size bill. Often perches more horizontally than a kingbird. Gray-washed face, grayish white below, pale yellow belly. Rusty patch on folded wing.

Cassin's Kingbird

Tyrannus vociferans

L 8.75" | **WS** 16"

Sometimes confused with the more widespread Western Kingbird, the Cassin's Kingbird is darker overall, with a rather dark gray breast and contrasting white throat. The Cassin's prefers oak savanna and the edge of open woodland rather than the more open habitats used by Westerns. This species is largely restricted to lower elevations along the Coastal Ranges, north to approximately the latitude of Gilroy. The Highway 101 corridor between Pismo Beach and Goleta is great Cassin's Kingbird country. Some retreat to the south in winter, but Cassin's Kingbirds can be seen all year round in California. The classic call is a rough-sounding *PHeeerrrr*; the song is an accelerating series of nasal notes.

Similar to Western Kingbird, but colors more saturated. Darker gray face and breast, white "beard," yellow belly. Tail with buffy tip; appears white-edged when backlit but not as boldly as in Western.

Western Kingbird

Tyrannus verticalis

L 8.5" | **WS** 15"

A species of wide-open grasslands and fields, the Western Kingbird nests on tall power poles and other structures almost throughout California, arriving in early March and leaving again by mid-October; breeders are absent only from the higher reaches of the Sierra and the desert southeast. Kingbirds are readily seen perched or flycatching along I-5 through the Central Valley. Diurnal migrants can be seen moving north along the coast in April; numbers also congregate in the Coachella Valley. The Western is paler than the similar Cassin's Kingbird, with a different voice. Most of the Western Kingbird's rollicking vocalizations sound like squeaky toys.

Pale gray head and breast without strong contrast to white throat. Pale yellow below; blackish tail with bold white edges to outer feathers.

Loggerhead Shrike

Lanius ludovicianus

L 8.5″ | **WS** 12″

This songbird behaves more like a small raptor, even hovering over lizards and small rodents like an American Kestrel. Prey is dispatched with the large, hooked bill; shrikes also use thorns or barbed wire to help kill their sometimes surprisingly large prey, which they may hang on a fence to eat later. This is a widespread but sadly declining year-round resident, largely absent from the forested northeast and the forests of the Sierra; more are found in winter, when migrants from the north arrive. Numbers can still be found in the lower San Joaquin, Imperial, and Panoche Valleys. Call is a rasping, descending *CHRRR Chrrr chrrrr.*

Perches horizontally. Big head with strong hooked beak. Gray, with bold black mask, wings, and long tail; paler below.

Bell's Vireo

Vireo bellii

L 4.5" | **WS** 7"

Once more widespread in the state, the Bell's Vireo is now a rare and declining breeder in shrubby riparian areas in southern California between Los Angeles and San Diego and in the Colorado River Valley; a few breed at isolated sites farther north. The Tijuana River Valley is a great place to look for this bird, which arrives by early April and leaves by mid-September, wintering in Mexico. Bell's Vireos in California are quite drab and grayish; they are smaller and slimmer than "typical" vireos. The distinctive song is a bouncing, musical jumble.

Small and slim with stout grayish bill; often raises tail. Grayish, lacking contrast; has only one (lower) narrow wing bar and longish legs.

Cassin's Vireo

Vireo cassinii

L 5″ | **WS** 9″

The Cassin's Vireo breeds in coniferous and mixed forests in the north of the state, in the Sierra, in the Coastal Ranges, and, less commonly, in some of the southern ranges; it moves south to Mexico in winter. East of the Sierra, the much more uniformly grayish Plumbeous Vireo is distinguished from the Cassin's by the white rather than yellowish edges to its wing feathers. The song of the Cassin's Vireo is a series of husky, throaty phrases, most ending in an upswing, a few dropping at the end. Alarm call a nasal descending scold *zh zh zh zh zp*.

Small, stocky bird with thick grayish bill. Large-headed; looks like it is wearing white spectacles. Gray head blends into whiter throat, both of which contrast with greener back.

Hutton's Vireo

Vireo huttoni

L 5″ | **WS** 8.25″

The most common and most widespread vireo in the state, the Hutton's Vireo is a permanent resident in most places, with some dispersal in fall and winter; this species is absent only from the desert, the floor of the Central Valley, and the arid areas east of the Sierra. Hutton's Vireos like oak woodlands, but will also inhabit riparian and mixed forests. They flock with chickadees and wintering warblers, and may serve as sentinels, alerting other birds with the loud alarm, a nasal *ree-dee dee dee*. The song is very monotonous, a single note repeated for minutes at a time before the bird switches to a different repeated note. The vocalizations help separate this vireo from the smaller, faster-moving Ruby-crowned Kinglet. The kinglet has a dark bar immediately behind the lower wing bar, lacking in the Hutton's.

Small and big-headed, with stocky bill. Olive green, paler below, white wing bars. Lower wing bar not bordered by dark bar as in similar Ruby-crowned Kinglet.

Warbling Vireo

Vireo gilvus

L 5″ | **WS** 8.75″

This nondescript vireo seems to be undergoing a long-term decline in California, but is still common in some areas. Warbling Vireos breed in the north, the Coast Ranges, the Transverse Mountains, the San Jacinto Mountains, and the Sierra; they occur as migrants elsewhere. Breeders inhabit open forest edge and riparian areas, particularly those with deciduous trees such as willows or cottonwoods. The song is a husky, run-on warble that ends with an upslurred note. Call is a nasal *nzzzaahh*.

Small and slim, nondescript. Bill larger and grayer than that of a warbler. Dull head pattern with paler eyebrow; beady dark eye stands out on face. Blue-gray legs.

Pinyon Jay

Gymnorhinus cyanocephalus

L 11" | **WS** 18"

This species of Great Basin pinyon-juniper forests ranges west to eastern California, where it is resident at lower elevations of the east slope of the Sierra from South Lake Tahoe south; there are also isolated populations in the San Bernardino and San Jacinto Mountains. Look for Pinyon Jays in early fall at Mono Lake County Park or Markleeville. Dependent on the seeds of pinyon pine, these jays may wander widely when that crop fails. They are found in flocks, sometimes numbering in the hundreds. The flight is powerful and steady, like a small crow. The nasal calls are a laughing *wayaa* or *waayayaa*.

Mid-size sky-blue jay with long, chisel-like bill.

Steller's Jay

Cyanocitta stelleri

L 12.5" | **WS** 17.25"

This forest-loving jay is a common and widespread permanent resident in California, most common on the moister central coast and in the north, and absent from the desert. An adaptable bird, Steller's Jays feed in trees or on the ground in tall, shady forests, campgrounds, and backyards. Hard to miss, they are usually found in pairs or noisy family groups. In flight, looks shorter-tailed, stockier, and darker than the Western Scrub-Jay. The primary calls are a harsh *charrrrrrr* and sharp *shek-shek-shek-shek*.

Conspicuously noisy large songbird with big expressive crest. Blue with browner head and neck. At close range shows blue eyebrows.

Island Scrub-Jay

Aphelocoma insularis

L 13″ | **WS** 16.75″

This jay is a permanent resident of Santa Cruz Island in the Channel Islands occurring nowhere else in the world. By taking a boat from Ventura Harbor, you can find this California endemic in the island's oak woodlands, on chaparral edges, and near the campsites and landing areas. The Island Scrub-Jay is larger and bigger-billed than its mainland relative, the Western Scrub-Jay; the plumage is darker, with blue on the undertail coverts. Voice similar to Western Scrub-Jay.

Only jay on Santa Cruz Island. Like Western Scrub-Jay but larger, with stouter bill, darker mask, and blue wash to undertail coverts.

Western Scrub-Jay

Aphelocoma californica

L 11.5" | **WS** 15.5"

Common and widespread in California, this noisy jay is a year-round resident of forest edges, chaparral, urban areas, and oak savanna; it is absent from the desert and densely forested areas in the north and Sierra. The population found east of the Sierra, at sites such as Lee Vining, is paler and less boldly marked, with blue on the undertail coverts; this "Woodhouse's Jay" may represent a separate species. Scrub-Jays are encountered in pairs or small groups, in more open areas than the Steller's Jay. Western Scrub-Jays give a nasal, strident *sheeeenk* call; the Woodhouse's Jay's voice is less raucous and lower-pitched.

Slim, long-tailed jay without a crest. Bill is thick. Blue on head, wings, tail, with ashy-gray back, darker mask, white throat bordered by blue half-collar.

Black-billed Magpie

Pica hudsonia

L 20.5″ | **WS** 23.5″

This hardy and adaptable species is a resident of grasslands, agricultural areas, sagebrush flats, and farmsteads east of the Sierra and north of the desert. Its range does not overlap with that of the Yellow-billed, which occurs west of the mountains. Found in small flocks, Black-billed Magpies feed on the ground, raising the long tail when alarmed. The calls include an inquisitive nasal *jeeeeenk* and a harsh, rapid *jak-jak-jak-jak*.

Large, elegant bird with a very long tail. Black with iridescent blue wings and tail, white belly. Bill entirely black.

Yellow-billed Magpie

Pica nuttalli

L 19″ | **WS** 24″

The Yellow-billed Magpie's worldwide range is essentially restricted to the ring of oak savanna around the Central Valley. This species occurs north to Redding; it is curiously absent from the southern end of the San Joaquin Valley, although it extends along the Coast Ranges to Santa Barbara. Yellow-billed Magpies are found in small flocks, usually near oaks, but they also commonly feed on agricultural land and pastures. Very closely related to the Black-billed Magpie, with essentially identical vocalizations. The calls include an inquisitive nasal *jeeeeenk* and a harsh, rapid *jak-jak-jak-jak*.

Large, elegant bird with a very long tail. Black with iridescent blue wings and tail, white belly. Bright yellow bill, and often yellow around eye.

American Crow

Corvus brachyrhynchos

L 18.5″ | **WS** 36.5″

Everyone knows the big, black, noisy crow. Rarer in the desert and east of the Sierra, small groups of American Crows can be seen in most of the state feeding on the ground or gathering at large roosts in the nonbreeding season. Some crows forage on the shore, but this intelligent and inquisitive bird is more commonly found in parking lots, agricultural areas, fields, and any open place with larger trees nearby for nesting. Crows are smaller and less aggressive-looking than ravens. The classic crowing *caaw* is supplemented with other sounds and rattles. Calling birds often flare the tail at each call.

All black, with strong black bill. Smaller, gentler-looking than Common Raven. Fan-shaped tail.

Common Raven

Corvus corax

L 24.5″ | **WS** 46″

The Common Raven is a huge, big-billed, and more hawk-like version of a crow. Ravens are much more powerful and acrobatic in flight than their smaller relatives; ravens often soar and glide, while crows tend to steadily beat their wings. Usually seen singly, in pairs, or in small family groups, ravens are particularly common in hilly or mountainous areas, at forest edges, in grasslands and agricultural fields, and even over dense forest. This species is resident throughout California, including the desert. The calls are throatier than those of a crow, including a loud, harsh *graaak* and various popping and gurgling noises.

All black. Larger than crow, with massive bill and short legs. Throat often looks shaggy.

All black. More raptor-like than crow. Wings somewhat pointed, tail wedge-shaped.

Clark's Nutcracker

Nucifraga columbiana

L 11" | **WS** 22"

Synonymous with the open conifer forests of the high mountains, the Clark's Nutcracker is an uncommon and intelligent resident of the Sierra, Mount Pinos, San Gabriel, San Bernardino, and San Jacinto Mountains. This species feeds mostly on pine seeds and caches them in many thousands of locations for the winter, which it recalls with amazing success. During particularly harsh weather or in times of food scarcity, nutcrackers may wander to lower elevations. The Angeles National Forest is a good place to look for them. The calls include a harsh *chhhaaaaakkkk!* and many other rattles, yelps, and chattering notes.

Almost crow-sized. Cold gray with long, black, spike-like bill. Contrasting black wings, black tail with white sides.

Horned Lark

Eremophila alpestris

L 7″ | **WS** 12.5″

The only native lark breeding in North America, this species is a resident of flat and open, often very sparse, habitats, from grasslands to agricultural fields; it is absent from higher areas of the Sierra and densely forested sites in the north and Coast Ranges. Horned Larks are terrestrial, with a unique long-winged, crouched, almost hunch-backed appearance on the ground. They walk rather than hop. California Horned Larks tend to be very warmly colored, almost reddish above and deep yellow below, sometimes with streaking on the flanks. Juveniles, seen in summer, lack the bold face pattern of adults, but can still be identified by their behavior and odd speckled look. The song is a beautiful high-pitched tinkling warble, more excited towards the end. Flight call a high *see-titi*.

Terrestrial; walks, does not hop. Pinkish brown above, complicated head pattern with black "horns." Black forehead, mask, and breast, yellowish throat.

Purple Martin

Progne subis

L 8″ | **WS** 16″

California's largest swallow is now rather rare, suffering from the removal of its nesting snags and the loss of suitable cavities to European Starlings. Its stronghold is in the northwest, but there are isolated populations in various mountain ranges, where martins still nest in large dead snags. There is also a population that nests under a freeway overpass near Sacramento. Loosely colonial, our martins do not use martin condos as they do in the East, but they will nest in single boxes or gourds. They arrive by late April and go south by August. Calls and songs are melodious and liquid.

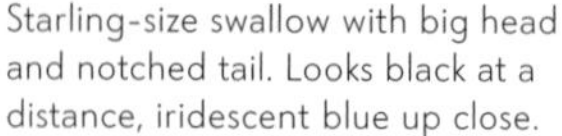

Starling-size swallow with big head and notched tail. Looks black at a distance, iridescent blue up close.

Female shiny blue above with gray collar and dark face; pale below, mottled on throat, flanks, and vent.

Tree Swallow

Tachycineta bicolor

L 5.25″ | **WS** 13″

This common swallow nests in tree cavities and nest boxes, usually but not always near water. Like the Violet-green, this swallow breeds in northern and central California and winters commonly in the central and southern part of the state; flocks hunt insects over ponds and wet fields, and tree swallows sometimes eat berries in winter. Outside of the breeding season, large roosts form in marshes or cornfields. Similar to the Violet-green, but the Tree Swallow's rump is largely dark, and the dark face is set off strongly from the white throat. Voice is pleasant liquid notes.

Swallow with fully bright white underparts. Dark iridescent blue to green above; face and rump both dark.

In flight, dark upperparts contrast with white underparts, particularly the throat. Female varies from brownish when young to dull shiny blue above.

Violet-green Swallow

Tachycineta thalassina

L 4.75" | **WS** 10.5"

A male Violet-green Swallow is an exceedingly beautiful bird, with a truly violet rump and a gorgeous grass-green back. The white wrap-around on the sides of the rump is distinctive in all plumages. With its fluttery flight and narrow wings, the Violet-green can sometimes suggest a White-throated Swift in flight. This western swallow breeds commonly in northern and central California, especially in montane habitats, and winters in central and southern California; winter flocks, which often include Tree Swallows, gather where aquatic insects are emerging. The Violet-green Swallow nests in natural cavities, but it has adapted well to people and will often nest in building crevices or under eaves. One call is an electric-sounding *tchew* or *pitchew*. Song is more hurried and rougher than in the Tree Swallow.

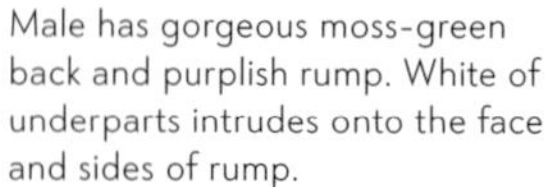

Male has gorgeous moss-green back and purplish rump. White of underparts intrudes onto the face and sides of rump.

In flight, dark upperparts contrast with white underparts, particularly the throat. Female varies from brownish when young to dull shiny blue above.

Northern Rough-winged Swallow

Stelgidopteryx serripennis

L 5″ | **WS** 11″

Widespread during the breeding season in California, this brown swallow is typically found in only small numbers, limited by its need for dirt banks to nest in. Typically found near water, it uses even rather small banks or dirt scrapes along a creek. Unlike the Bank Swallow, this species is not colonial. Arrives in California in March and leaves by September, wintering mainly in Mexico and Central America. Like other swallows, it catches its insect prey in the air. Its longer, more swept-back wings give it a looser flight style than other swallows. Juveniles have neat cinnamon wing bars. The voice is a gravelly *phrrrtt*.

A brownish swallow with white belly and vent. Dirty brown extends to breast and throat.

Brownish above and white below, throat and breast with buffy wash.

Bank Swallow

Riparia riparia

L 5″ | **WS** 10.5″

Rare and local in California, this colonial nester is officially listed as threatened in the state. The nesting colonies, in earthen banks on the coast or along rivers, range from dozens to hundreds of birds; look for Bank Swallows at Fort Funston in San Francisco or Año Nuevo Reserve in San Mateo County. Migrants can be found in March and August anywhere swallows congregate. Sometimes confused with the Northern Rough-winged Swallow, but look for the white throat and discrete dark band on the breast. Call is an almost insect-like buzz, drier and shorter than the call of a Northern Rough-winged Swallow.

Brown swallow with white underparts and neat brown breast band.

In flight, small and brown above, with noticeable brown breast band on white underparts.

Cliff Swallow

Petrochelidon pyrrhonota

L 5″ | **WS** 11.5″

Ubiquitous during the breeding season, sometimes nesting by the hundreds beneath freeway overpasses, Cliff Swallows arrive in March and leave by September. This is the species famous for its arrival at the San Juan de Capistrano mission. Cliff Swallows originally nested on cliffs, but now almost all nests are secured to human-made structures. The mud nest is globular with a circular entrance on the side; a new nest is constructed every year. The song is soft, with an unpleasant creaking, screechy quality. The flight call is a low *pheeurr.*

Ornate swallow with chestnut face, blackish cap, and contrasting white forehead. Dark above with rusty rump. Off-white below, with dark throat, gray on flanks. Stocky and square-tailed in flight.

Bulky-bodied with square-tipped tail; tawny rump contrasts with dark back. Dark face with white forehead and chestnut throat.

Barn Swallow

Hirundo rustica

L 6.5" | **WS** 12"

The common name of this highly migratory species refers to its habit of nesting on buildings, porches, and bridges; it is now almost impossible to find a Barn Swallow building its cup-shaped mud and grass nest away from a man-made structure. Barn Swallows arrive in California in March and leave by October; on warm late-winter days, some can be seen migrating north along the coast. The song is quick and stuttering, with buzzy and liquid notes. Call is a low *vit*.

Slim swallow with long forked tail. Rusty forehead and throat merge into cinnamon underparts. Head and upperparts black with blue iridescence.

Slim. Forked tail with white band halfway to tip. Buffy to cinnamon below, glossy blue above.

Oak Titmouse

Baeolophus inornatus

L TK" | **WS** TK"

The adaptable Oak Titmouse is resident over most of California, except where its preferred oak woodlands are missing, as in the Sierra, the northeast, and parts of the central coast. Found in backyards and forests alike, titmice sometimes travel in the company of White-breasted Nuthatches. The similar Juniper Titmouse can be found at some sites east of the Sierra. Titmice have a pleasant repeated song of whistled phrases, *twee-dleee twee-dleee*.... The typical call is a set of soft notes followed by a harsher note, *tsi tsi tsi churrr.*

In flocks in oak habitats. Stocky and small, grayish but paler below. Noticeable crest, peg-like bill with blue-gray base.

Mountain Chickadee

Poecile gambeli

L 4.5″ | **WS** 8.25″

Absent from the coastal mountains in the central section of the state, the non-migratory Mountain Chickadee is otherwise common in California's open, dry montane conifer forests from the far northern Sierra to the southern ranges. Nests in cavities like other chickadees. A common feeder bird, this species moves downslope in winter. The pale eyebrow gives the Mountain Chickadee an aggressive impression. The song is a pleasing series of short whistles, often three, with the first higher-pitched: *fwee tiuu tiuu*. The call is *chica-dzee dzee*.

White eyebrow imparts mischievous look. Pale cheek, black cap, and black throat of typical chickadee; grayish body, paler below.

Chestnut-backed Chickadee

Poecile rufescens

L 4.25" | **WS** 7.5"

This adaptable resident is common at backyard feeders and in old deciduous and coniferous forests in the Coastal Ranges and northern Sierra. These chickadees sometimes use nest boxes. They often form the nucleus of mixed flocks, joined by warblers in migration and by Hutton's Vireos, Bushtits, and Ruby-crowned Kinglets in winter. North of the Golden Gate, these chickadees have more chestnut on the flanks, while the flanks of more southerly birds are gray. Song not often heard; the call is a very muffled and high-pitched *tsi-chee* or a longer *tsi tsi chee chee*.

Cute-faced chickadee with chestnut back, black cap and throat, white cheeks. Flanks gray in south, chestnut in north.

Verdin

Auriparus flaviceps

L 4″ | **WS** 8.25″

The sharp-billed Verdin is a tiny but striking bird of the desert, the adult gray with a bright yellow head and chestnut shoulders. Juveniles are dull gray, and can be confused with the Lucy's Warbler, which has a rusty rump. A resident of the deserts of the southeast, the Verdin can be common in towns and suburbs with abundant ornamental vegetation such as Palm Springs. It moves quickly through mesquites and other desert shrubs and trees, looking feverishly for insect prey in the leaves. The sharp *tcheef* call is often heard, as is a pleasant *tee–too* or *tee–too–too*.

Tiny, grayish desert bird with yellow head; chestnut shoulders can be concealed.

Nondescript juvenile brownish gray with beady eye on featureless face, sharply pointed bill.

Bushtit

Psaltriparus minimus

L 3″ | **WS** 6″

For much of the year, bushtits travel in flocks of twenty or more, marauding armies of miniature birds in search of tiny insects and spiders in the foliage. They split up into pairs for the breeding season, when they build an amazing hanging nest held together with spider webs and nicely camouflaged in a bush or tree. A common resident throughout the state, the Bushtit will explore any shrubby or edge habitat, including backyards. Birds east of the Sierra are more grayish, with gray crowns. The call is a high-pitched *tzee*, becoming a cacophony of high-pitched notes when given by a flock. A louder, longer buzzy trill is given as an alarm when a raptor is nearby.

Tiny, long-tailed, grayish bird with large head and peg-like bill. Brown-capped in most of California, more grayish east of Sierra. Males have dark eyes, females yellow.

White-breasted Nuthatch

Sitta carolinensis

L 5.25″ | **WS** 9.25″

The White-breasted is the largest of California's nuthatches. The state's two resident populations may represent two different species. In the Bay Area, around the rim of the Central Valley, and south to southern California, birds have a nasal *nyeaaa* call and occur in oaks. The slightly longer-billed population inhabiting conifers in the Sierra and east of the mountains has a machine-gun-like *dadadadadada*. Like all nuthatches, White-breasted creeps headfirst down tree trunks and finds food by probing the bark with its slightly upturned bill.

White face; male's cap is black, female's gray; blue-gray upperparts with whitish underparts and hint of reddish on vent. Long, slightly upturned bill.

Red-breasted Nuthatch

Sitta canadensis

L 4.25" | **WS** 7.5"

Specializing in conifer seeds, the colorful Red-breasted Nuthatch breeds in the north, in the Sierra, and in the higher reaches of the coastal and southern mountains. In years when cones are scarce to our north, large numbers migrate into the state's coniferous habitats, where they form mixed flocks with chickadees. This inquisitive species is often responsive to "pishing" by humans to draw them closer for viewing. The call is a short, high-pitched *yank*.

A small nuthatch with bold white eyebrow. Blue-gray above, rusty below with white throat. Male with black crown, female with gray.

Pygmy Nuthatch

Sitta pygmaea

L 4" | **WS** 8"

This smallest of the nuthatches is resident in much of California, except for the far northeast, the desert, and the Central Valley. Pygmy Nuthatches are partial to tall, dry pine forests, but they are also at home in introduced eucalyptus and cypress. They are usually found in noisy flocks, giving short, nasal "squeaky toy" piping calls. They can be hard to see high in the trees, but in some areas they come to bird feeders. Look for the Pygmy's lack of a pale eyebrow and the brownish gray crown with a small white spot on the nape.

The smallest of our nuthatches, round-bodied and short-tailed. Head with brownish crown and darker mask; creamy white below, blue-gray above.

Brown Creeper

Certhia americana

L 5″ | **WS** 7.25″

Unlike the headfirst clambering of the nuthatches, the Brown Creeper crawls up tree trunks, probing for insects with its thin and slightly down-curved bill. Once the bird reaches the top of the tree, it flies down to start again low on a new trunk. Creepers are found in all types of forest, most commonly in tall coastal trees such as redwood and Douglas-fir. The nest is hidden in a crevice or behind loose bark. This species is resident in much of California, but largely absent from the floor of the Central Valley. Creepers have a very high-pitched *seeee* that can be confused with the multi-syllabled call of the Golden-crowned Kinglet. The song is sweet and pleasant, rather musical for such an unassuming bird.

Creeps up trees, where it looks like a moving piece of bark. Thin downcurved bill, pale eyebrow and underparts, cryptic pattern above.

Rock Wren

Salpinctes obsoletus

L 5.25" | **WS** 9"

Resident over much of the state, except the north coast and the floor of the Central Valley. Migrants from the north and east of us do show up in winter in areas where this wren does not breed. However its breeding distribution is patchy, it can occur in isolated rocky spots such as the lighthouse in Point Reyes, Devil's Slide Park south of Pacifica in the Bay Area, or rocky areas in South Tufa in Mono Lake. This well-named wren occupies open rocky slopes in mountainous areas, often found together with the larger and rusty colored Canyon Wren. The far-carrying call is a rasping *ptzeee*. The song is made up of repeated ringing phrases with a buzzy quality, *beazz beazz bezoo bezooo....*

Rocky habitats; does not usually cock tail like relatives. Grayish, paler below with cinnamon on lower flanks; obscure mottling above and on throat. Downcurved bill, strongly barred undertail coverts.

Canyon Wren

Catherpes mexicanus

L 5″ | **WS** 7.5″

A well-named bird, this boldly patterned wren prefers cliffs and vertical canyon walls. Resident but patchily distributed in its habitat, the Canyon Wren is more common in the southern and eastern parts of the state; look for it in the Angeles National Forest or in the Bay Area's Del Puerto Canyon Road. When you hear the gorgeous cascading song, falling in pitch and ending with nasal buzzes, look on a big boulder or cliff top for the wren's bright white throat. The call is simpler than the song, a *jeenk* higher-pitched and more strident than the Rock Wren's call.

Large, thickset wren of rocky canyons. Rufous throughout with contrasting white throat and breast. Long downcurved bill with yellow lower mandible. Rufous tail with narrow dark bars.

House Wren

Troglodytes aedon

L 4.75" | **WS** 6"

This common wren of edge habitats and backyards breeds throughout the state; it is migratory in the east and north and along the coast, but resident from the mid-coast south. It is usually found in more rural habitats than the Bewick's Wren and in drier, more open habitats than the Pacific Wren. Males build many nests, one of which is eventually selected by the female; the others are "dummy nests." Such nests can keep other species from using nest boxes. House Wrens sing a bubbly series of trills and buzzes. The call is a buzzy *phhrreww,* like a finger being run over a comb.

Small, dull, pale brownish wren; often cocks tail. Slightly downcurved bill creates frowning expression. Beady eye stands out on dull face; dull barring throughout.

Bewick's Wren

Thryomanes bewickii

L 5″ | **WS** 7″

The expected backyard wren in much of the state, this resident species also occupies areas of riparian shrubs, chaparral, and forest edge. It is more locally distributed in the far north and the desert. Birds east of the Sierras and in the desert are slightly more grayish than those from coastal slope populations. Overlaps in some areas with the House Wren, but the white eyebrow stripe and tail with white and black barred corners identify the Bewick's. Song is buzzier and more emphatic than the Song Sparrow's, with more staccato and mechanical notes. Calls include scolding buzzes, raspy notes, a *churr,* and a *chip*.

Slim wren with long tail; brown above, pale and unmarked below. Obvious whitish eyebrow. Underside of tail white with dark bars.

Pacific Wren

Troglodytes pacificus

L 4″ | **WS** 5.5″

Pacific Wrens are a species of very moist, dark forests, often near creeks or streams. They like areas with dense fern cover, usually under conifers, and are most abundant in the shady forests of the north coast, where they can be one of the most frequently encountered species. They breed south to Big Sur on the coast and to the southern Sierra. Their migration is not well understood, but some are seen in winter away from the breeding areas on the southern coast slope. For a tiny bird, this wren has a loud and beautiful voice. The complex song is long and varied, a high-pitched, warbling mix of buzzy notes and sweet trills. The calls include a doubled *tchat-tchat* that can recall the call of a Wilson's Warbler, and a dry, machine-gun-like trill.

Tiny wren; rufous brown with narrow pale eyebrow. Round body and short, cocked tail.

Marsh Wren

Cistothorus palustris

L 4.75" | **WS** 6.75"

This wren of tule and cattail marshes breeds commonly on the coast, in the Central Valley, and in the marshes of the east slope and desert; it is mostly absent from forested and mountainous areas. This is usually the only wren expected in a marsh, but it can also be found in thick shrubbery near water in the winter, when the species seems more widespread and more numerous, probably thanks to migrants from the north. Marsh Wrens are not necessarily shy, but the dense habitat can make them difficult to see; look for the strong rusty tones, pale eyebrow, and striped back. They take a conspicuous perch to belt out their variable song, which includes dry trills, *tik–tik trrrr* or *chip-chi-dldldldld*. The call is a buzzy *chzz*.

Wetlands. Brown-capped wren with pale eyebrow; brown upperparts with black and white striped back. Paler below, buffy wash on flanks.

Cactus Wren

Campylorhynchus brunneicapillus

L 8″ | **WS** 11″

This very large wren is as notable for its personality as for its affinity with desert cacti, often nesting in cholla or other cactus species. Somewhat terrestrial, though it also forages higher in vegetation, this species is common in Joshua Tree National Park. A different form, with a more clearly spotted breast and paler underparts than the interior birds, occurs in coastal sage scrub between Ventura and San Diego Counties, with its highest numbers in Orange County. The song is far from musical, a repetitive rolling set of notes *rrr rrr rrr rrr,* sometimes with a more liquid tone. Call notes are metallic clicks and rasps.

Big, thick-billed wren. Ornate, with a brown cap and white eyebrow stripe; brown above with pale streaks, speckled on white and buffy background below.

Blue-gray Gnatcatcher

Polioptila caerulea

L 4″ | **WS** 6.25″

A tiny bird with a long and expressive tail, the Blue-gray Gnatcatcher is widespread in California, except in the higher mountains, densely forested areas, and the interior of the desert. A species of dry chaparral, thickets, shrubby areas, and oak woodland edges, it is generally uncommon, but more abundant in winter in the southern third of the state; small numbers winter north to the Bay Area, with higher densities from Morro Bay south on the coastal slope. All vocalizations are nasal, with a kissing quality. The song sounds disorganized, short slurred notes interspersed with buzzy kissing sounds. The common call is a nasal, falling *zheeewww*.

Tiny and slim, with long white-edged tail that looks entirely white from below. Blue-gray above, pale below; male has black eyebrow.

Female lacks black eyebrow; white eye ring more obvious than on male.

California Gnatcatcher

Polioptila californica

L 4″ | **WS** 5.5″

A relatively rare little bird and a true California specialty, this species is restricted to coastal sage scrub from the Los Angeles basin south to San Diego and across the border into Baja. Urbanization has fragmented what was once its expansive range, and the coastal population is federally listed as threatened. Look for it in Los Angeles in the Montebello Hills and on Palos Verdes Peninsula, or in the Tijuana River estuary at San Elijo Lagoon and Border Field State Park. Listen for the cat-like, nasal mewing, *mzzeewww mzzeewww.*

A dark gnatcatcher of the southern coastal slope. Tail largely black from below; male has a black cap.

A dark gnatcatcher of the southern coastal slope. Tail largely black from below; female has a white eye ring, buffy wash on rear flank.

Black-tailed Gnatcatcher

Polioptila melanura

L 4″ | **WS** 5.5″

The Black-tailed is the non-migratory gnatcatcher of the desert, moving around in shrubby areas and scrub, in summer often in pairs or family groups. It is restricted to the desert southeast, where it is uncommon. The Black-tailed has a darker tail and is dirtier gray than the Blue-gray Gnatcatcher; the male acquires a full black cap in the breeding season. The calls recall the scold of a House Wren, *chhhh chhhh chhh chhh chhh*; the *pzeee* note is harsher than the corresponding call of the Blue-gray.

Desert, east of mountains. Pale gnatcatcher with largely black undertail; male has black cap and white eye ring.

Largely black undertail. Female lacks cap of male; similar to female Blue-gray Gnatcatcher but back has brownish wash.

Golden-crowned Kinglet

Regulus satrapa

L 3.75″ | **WS** 6.25″

Resident in the north, the Sierra, and the forests of the Coastal Ranges, the Golden-crowned Kinglet is closely associated with tall coniferous forests, where it can be difficult to see high in the trees. The Golden-crowned visits the rest of the state in migration or winter, when it sometimes flocks with chickadees and the similar-sounding Brown Creeper. Up close, the Golden-crowned Kinglet is an exotic-looking little bird; only the male has the hidden orange patch in the yellow crown. The song starts with a high-pitched series, followed by a sneezy chatter that recalls a chickadee. Calls are high-pitched and very similar to the Brown Creeper's, but given in twos or threes, *zee zee zee*.

Tiny bird of conifers, with black crown and white eyebrow. Golden to orange crown patch. Greenish above, paler below, wing with dark stripe across yellow-edged primaries.

Ruby-crowned Kinglet

Regulus calendula

L 4" | **WS** 6.75"

The Ruby-crowned Kinglet nests in low densities in the Sierra and the highest parts of the southern mountains. Migrants occur in various habitats, but not usually coniferous trees; they flock with chickadees and wintering warblers, and can be seen with the lookalike Hutton's Vireo. The kinglet is more active than the vireo, and has black legs, a thinner bill, and a black line bordering the lower wing bar. Rarely, when a male is excited he will reveal the hidden ruby patch in the crown; count yourself lucky if you see this. Frequently calls when flocking, a dry chatter *cht cht cht*. The song, often heard on the spring migration, is a long, varied sequence beginning with high-pitched notes and ending with a lively warble.

Tiny green bird with white eye ring. Similar to Hutton's Vireo, but has black bar behind lower wing bar, black legs with yellow feet.

Wrentit

Chamaea fasciata

L 5.75″ | **WS** 7″

Most of the Wrentit's range is in California. This is the most resolutely resident of our birds, over its entire lifetime rarely moving even a mile from where it hatched. Absent from the desert and east of the Sierra, Wrentits are chaparral specialists, occupying poison oak thickets and, in the north, salal shrubs. They are territorial year round. The male gives an accelerating bouncing-ball song, while the female's song does not speed up at the end. The call is a dry *chrrrtt*.

Difficult to see in dense chaparral. Long tail often cocked. Brown body with grayer head, warm pinkish wash to throat; yellow eyes.

American Dipper

Cinclus mexicanus

L 6.75″ | **WS** 11″

The sturdy-bodied dipper is an entirely aquatic songbird, swimming and diving in rushing streams, then popping up on a rock, looking dry and pristine. Resident in the Sierra and Coast Ranges and mountains in the south, dippers eat the larvae of stoneflies, mayflies, and other aquatic insects. They like to perch, constantly bobbing, on big rocks mid-stream; white-wash-covered rocks are a good clue that dippers are in the area. The call, often given in flight, is a buzzy *dzert*. The beautiful song is musical and varied.

A rotund gray bird of creeks and rivers, with short paddle-like wings and short tail. White "eyelid" obvious when the bird blinks.

Mountain Bluebird

Sialia currucoides

L 7.25" | **WS** 13.25"

A species of mountain meadows and California's east slope, some mountain bluebirds move west in winter to such Central Valley sites as Sutter Buttes, or rarely even to the coast. Highway 33 in the Cuyama area can have large wintertime concentrations. Our two bluebird species can be found together; while their feeding habits are similar, the Mountain Bluebird inhabits more open areas with fewer perches, forcing it to hover more. Flight call a *tweew,* higher pitched than Western Bluebird.

Seems longer than the Western Bluebird. Male gorgeous sky-blue with slightly more grayish underparts and white vent.

Slimmer than Western Bluebird. Female grayish with white eye ring, blue wings and tail. Long wings extend almost to tail tip.

Western Bluebird

Sialia mexicana

L 7″ | **WS** 12.5″

Bluebirds are insectivores, usually seen quietly scanning from a fence post or wire or momentarily hovering before dropping to pounce on their prey. The Western Bluebird can be found throughout the state; it is largely resident, although some move to the far south in winter. "Bluebird trails" created in agricultural and grassland areas have helped prop up the numbers of these attractive cavity-nesters. The spotted juveniles look quite different from the adults. The commonly heard call is a nasal *pfeeew*.

Found in open areas. Upright stance. Male is a blue bird with rusty breast, flanks, and back. Blue wings and tail, no wing bars.

Female duller than male, grayish with blue wings and tail; rusty back, breast, and flanks.

American Robin

Turdus migratorius

L 9.5" | **WS** 14"

This classic backyard bird is widespread in California during the breeding season, absent only from the deserts. It is much more common in winter, particularly in the south, when flocks switch from feeding on lawns to harvesting berries in trees or shrubs. Found in open forest, edge, shrubby thickets, urban areas, riparian streams, and oak woodlands. Juveniles can be confusing with their spotting above and below. The song is a sweet, melodious series with noticeable pauses between each phrase. The call is a throaty *triik!*, the alarm call a quavering *ja ja ja jau*.

Familiar. Orange-red breast, dark head, and striped throat. Male bright below, dark above, with bright yellow bill.

Female averages paler on breast, with paler, grayer head and duller bill. Still obviously orange-red on breast.

Juvenile spotted with dark below, but has some rusty. Also pale spots above. The shape is identical to that of the adult.

Varied Thrush

Ixoreus naevius

L 8.75" | **WS** 14.25"

Varied Thrushes like shade. They breed in the moist, dark forests of northwestern California, wintering in dark, moist sites throughout the state. Winter numbers vary from year to year, depending on food supplies farther north. In some places, the best time to see this species is before sunrise, when birds emerge to feed in open areas such as roads before returning to the deep darkness. In flight, Varied Thrushes show an orange underwing stripe and are shorter-tailed than robins. The song is a single ethereal whistle, repeated after a long pause, often on a different pitch. The call is like a Hermit Thrush's, a low *chuck*.

Male gorgeous orange below with blackish breast band, blackish head, and orange eyebrow. Orange-patterned wings.

Female duller, grayish head and breast band. Has orange eyebrow and orange-patterned wings.

Townsend's Solitaire

Myadestes townsendi

L 8.25" | **WS** 13.25"

A slim, quiet thrush that often sits still for long periods, usually at the top of a tree, the Townsend's Solitaire breeds in the mountain forests of the north, the Sierra, and southern California ranges. It winters at lower elevations in those areas, with some dispersal to other parts of the state. Solitaires nest in dirt banks in open coniferous forests. The song sounds like a speeded-up American Robin's, but with a bouncing quality and almost no spaces between phrases. The call note is a hollow *pheep,* with the quality of air blowing over a bottle.

Slim, with upright stance, tiny bill, and small head. All gray with white eye ring and buffy primary bases. Obvious buffy wing stripe in flight.

Swainson's Thrush

Catharus ustulatus

L 7" | **WS** 11.75"

The highly migratory Swainson's Thrush arrives in California in April and May; it breeds in the Coastal Ranges and the northern half of the state. All leave in winter, when the similar Hermit Thrush is common. Swainson's Thrushes nest in deciduous, often riparian forest, where they are easiest to see early in the season when singing to defend territory. Singing birds perch in view, but otherwise this is a shy and retiring species. Often found feeding on berries in fall. The gorgeous song is outdone only by the Hermit Thrush. Flutelike and ethereal, it begins hesitantly and rises at the end: *phew phew phew weuu weeuuweeuweuu*.... The calls include a loud piping *pheeep* and a rasping, cat-like *pk-meehhha*.

Russet above, but may look olive in dim light. Buffy eye ring connects to bill like eyeglasses. Warm-toned breast with dark spots.

Uniformly russet-toned from head to tail. Eyeglass look; warm-toned cheeks and breast sides.

Hermit Thrush

Catharus guttatus

L 6.25" | **WS** 10.5"

The common and widespread spotted thrush of winter, this species also breeds in high-elevation coniferous forests in the Sierra, the north, and the Coastal Ranges. Similar to the Swainson's Thrush, but Hermit Thrushes regularly twitch the tail up and droop the wings nervously, particularly after landing. Feeds on the ground, but in fall and winter also eats berries from trees and shrubs. The gorgeous three-parted, flute-like song begins with an even whistle, then warbles its way up or down in pitch to the ending phrases *sweee twedle twedle, phoooo weeoo weeoo*...; the initial note of the next song is at a slightly different pitch. Calls include a dry *chup* and a rising *sweee?*

Often droops wings and half-cocks tail. Olive-brown above, with contrasting rusty tail and wing edging. Pale eye ring not connected to bill. Extensive spotting below.

Rusty tail, extensive dark spotting below, pale eye ring that is not connected to bill.

Northern Mockingbird

Mimus polyglottos

L 9.25″ | **WS** 13″

A very adaptable bird of shrubby edge habitats and suburbs, this year-round resident is common in backyards, where it is often maligned for its habit of singing loudly in the middle of the night; those nocturnal songsters are apparently young, unmated males. Its famous ability to imitate voices gives this species its names. It feeds on berries during the fall and winter, and may defend a good source not only from other mocking-birds but also from thrushes and robins. The long, varied song includes much mimicry in its phrases, which are often repeated twice. The call is a low, dry *chup*.

Adult slim and long-tailed, grayish with dark through eye. Whitish wing bars and white patch at base of primaries. In flight, white patch on wings and much white on tail edge.

Juvenile with brown wash, yellow gape on bill, light spotting on breast.

Sage Thrasher

Oreoscoptes montanus

L 8.5" | **WS** 12.5"

Our only migratory thrasher, this species breeds in sagebrush east of the Sierra; some winter in the southwest portion of the state, though most head to Mexico. The long wings reflect its migratory habits. Perhaps because it breeds in such dry, dusty, sunny habitats, the Sage Thrasher's plumage wears and fades over the summer to look dull and low-contrast, but after the fall molt, it is once again fresh, crisp, and well spotted. The song is jumbled and hurried, often lacking the repeated notes typical of thrashers and more like a speeded-up thrush song. Call is a low *chup,* similar to that of the Hermit Thrush.

Like a streaky, short-tailed mockingbird. Short-billed thrasher with dull face and yellow eye. Streaked below to flanks; long wings, white tail corners in flight.

California Thrasher

Toxostoma redivivum

L 12.5" | **WS** 12.25"

The California Thrasher is another specialty almost entirely restricted to our state. A thrasher of chaparral and woodland edges, it occurs around the rim of the Central Valley, in coastal chaparral, and in scrub in the southwest. Shy and retiring when it feeds on the ground, this species is easiest to see in late winter and early spring, when territorial birds sing from conspicuous perches. Darker plumage, brown eye, and different habitat than the closely related Crissal Thrasher. Song may recall a Northern Mockingbird's but is rougher, with fewer repetitions and no mimicry. The call is an alarmed *pit-dik!*

A dark thrasher with long, downcurved bill. Face with dark eye-line and dark eye. Gray below, shading to buffy on belly and vent.

Crissal Thrasher

Toxostoma crissale

L 11.75″ | **WS** 12.5″

Found in washes and mesquite scrub in California's southeast deserts. The refuges in the Imperial Valley are good spots to see this often reclusive ground-feeder; it is more conspicuous when it perches up to sing in late winter and early spring. Essentially no overlap with the very similar California Thrasher. The Crissal has a pale eye, is much more grayish, and has a distinctly rufous crissum. The varied song of soft phrases interspersed with short *quip* notes is similar to the California Thrasher's, but sweeter and perhaps more mockingbird-like. Calls include an excited *pi-diu-diu*.

A pale thrasher with long, downcurved bill. Pale eye with no dark eye-line. Rusty undertail coverts contrast with brownish gray body.

Le Conte's Thrasher

Toxostoma lecontei

L 10.25" | **WS** 12"

Frequenting even drier, more sparsely-vegetated areas than the Crissal Thrasher, this uncommon and secretive bird is sometimes seen running, tail cocked high, across the bare ground of desert washes or creosote and saltbush flats. It is a year-round resident of the southeastern desert, but also occurs rarely in isolated dry pockets of the southern San Joaquin Valley. Usually difficult to see, these thrashers are most visible when they are singing in late winter and early spring. The rarer Bendire's Thrasher, a local resident in the north of our desert zone, is shorter-billed and spotted below. The song of the Le Conte's Thrasher has a mellower tempo than the other southern thrashers, with repetitions and sweet notes. The rising *wheep!* call recalls a Myiarchus flycatcher such as Brown-crested.

Slim, pale sandy thrasher, smaller than Crissal. Face has dark eye and masked look. Tawny undertail coverts do not contrast strongly with sandy brown body.

American Pipit

Anthus rubescens

L 6″ | **WS** 10.5″

The only pipit easily found in California, the American Pipit typically bobs its rear end continuously as it walks and feeds. Very terrestrial, this is not a bird you will ever see perched in a tree. A few breed in the very highest-elevation alpine areas of the Sierra, but pipits are mainly migrants and winter visitors in California, found all across our state. During the breeding season they are grayish above with a warm tawny coloration below, more colorful than in fall and winter. Long-tailed in flight, when they typically give a high-pitched call *tsip-tsip*.

Terrestrial, bobs rear end. Thin bill, unlike sparrows. Streaked below but not above. White edges on tail in flight.

European Starling

Sturnus vulgaris

L 8.5" | **WS** 14"

One of the most successful introduced species in North America, the starling is now a widespread and common resident of California's urban and agricultural habitats, breeding in nooks in buildings or bridges. Preferring edges, this species is absent from densely forested areas and high elevations, but it is found in desert towns. The spotted birds of winter look very different in spring, when the pale spots have worn away to reveal the darker, iridescent bases of the feathers. In summer the bill is yellow, with the base bluer in males and pinker in females. Songs are extremely varied and complex, gurgling and disorganized, and often including mimicry; Western Meadowlark song is a favorite ingredient. The varied calls include whistles and chatters.

Black at a distance, with long yellow bill. Stocky and short-tailed. In breeding plumage, glossy and exotic-looking pointed throat feathers.

In winter, body feathering tipped buffy, creating a thoroughly spotted look. Bill dark, wing feathers edged cinnamon.

In summer, juveniles drab gray with whitish throat and masked look. Become patchy blackish as they molt into adult-like plumage.

Cedar Waxwing

Bombycilla cedrorum

L 6″ | **WS** 10.25″

Cedar Waxwings are curious in several ways: their plumage is so smooth as to make the individual feathers indiscernible, they have odd red "wax" tips to the secondary feathers (presumably to attract mates), and they are songbirds with no song. A winter visitor all across California, waxwings also breed in open forests and on woodland edges in the far north. Their winter range and abundance vary from year to year; we see fewer when berries, their staple food, are plentiful to our north. The high-pitched *chreee* call is essentially their only vocalization.

Tawny head with shaggy crest and well-defined black mask. Grayish wings, tail, and rump; yellow tip to tail, red "sealing wax" spots on tips of secondary feathers.

Phainopepla

Phainopepla nitens

L 7.75″ | **WS** 11.5″

Related to the Cedar Waxwing and similarly crested, the much longer, slimmer Phainopepla feeds almost exclusively on mistletoe berries, and is found only in hotter, drier habitats where mistletoe grows, whether in mesquite woodlands in the desert or oak woodlands at the edge of the Central Valley. Resident in their California range, some Phainopepla withdraw from northern latitudes in winter. They are not found on the coast or in the Sierra. The song is soft warbled phrases that sound disjointed, with some harsh and some musical sections. Gives a low upslurred whistle, *hoeet*.

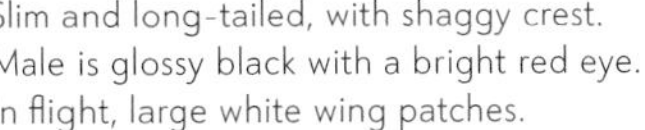

Slim and long-tailed, with shaggy crest. Male is glossy black with a bright red eye. In flight, large white wing patches.

Female like male with long tail, shaggy crest, with red eye, but grayish brown overall.

Orange-crowned Warbler

Oreothlypis celata

L 5" | **WS** 7.5"

Orange-crowned Warblers are one of our most widespread and common warblers. They breed throughout the state except the desert, and are common in winter in the more temperate coastal areas and lowlands of the south and Central Valley. Breeders inhabit chaparral and edge shrubbery and thickets, including high mountain meadows. Wintering birds occur in shrubbery and edge habitats with trees such as willows that retain their leaves. Our breeding birds are bright and yellowish, but in winter and migration we may see more northern birds, yellowish bodied with a grayish head, or even more eastern individuals, which are dull and grayish. The song is a trill, usually falling at the end. The call is a sharp *chip*.

Orange crown usually hidden. Sharply pointed bill. Dark eye line imparts serious expression. Breeding male yellowish below, greener above, with yellow undertail coverts.

Fall birds duller, yellowish below, greener above. Sharp bill, dark eye line, and pale crescents around eyes. Brightest yellow on undertail coverts.

Some distinctly grayish headed fall birds may be from northern or eastern populations. Dark eye-line, crescents around eye, and yellow undertail coverts.

Lucy's Warbler

Oreothlypis luciae

L 4" | **WS** 6.75"

The Lucy's is the desert warbler, with a marked preference for mesquite thickets in riparian areas. In California it breeds only in the far southeast, especially in the Colorado River Valley; a few rare individuals sometimes wander to the coast in fall. Lucy's is a little warbler with a sharply pointed bill and rusty rump. In the desert, it can be confused with the equally small and grayish juvenile Verdin, but the Lucy's always has some rusty on the rump and is a bit buffier on the underparts. The song is a high trill that changes in pitch halfway through. The call is a sharp *chik*.

Tiny gray warbler with pointy bill and white eye ring. Male darker gray, bold rusty crown and rump.

Female and fall birds duller, tiny, gray with pale face and white eye ring. Rusty rump.

Virginia's Warbler

Oreothlypis virginiae

L 4" | **WS** 7.5"

The Virginia's may look more like a Lucy's Warbler, but it is more closely related to the Nashville Warbler. Unlike the Nashville, it has gray wings, and the yellow of the underparts is restricted to the breast and vent. Not common in California, Virginia's Warblers nest only in thickets, riparian areas, or scrubby montane edges east of the Sierra, above the sagebrush zone. They are more frequent in migration, with a few found in fall in coastal areas. A behavioral clue is the constant tail-wagging as they feed in the trees. The song is a warble, sometimes loosely trilled, that changes pitch two or three times. Call a sharp *chik*.

Grayish warbler with white eye ring. Whitish below with yellow breast patch and undertail coverts. Male brighter, with rusty crown patch.

Females and immature duller, yellow on breast not obvious. Gray with white eye ring and yellow undertail coverts. May show rusty crown.

Nashville Warbler

Oreothlypis ruficapilla

L 4.25″ | **WS** 7.25″

Nashville Warblers breed mostly on the west slope of the Sierra and in the north; they migrate throughout California, less commonly on the coast. They twitch the tail, but not as consistently as the Virginia's. As you would expect from a bird named for country's Music City, it has a pretty song, a series of repeated whistles that change to a slightly more warbled phrase. Call a sharp *chik*.

Small warbler with pointy bill. Gray head contrasts with yellow throat, bold white eye ring. Greenish above including wings, yellow below.

Females and immature duller; yellow on throat, breast, and undertail coverts. Similar to Virginia's, but greenish wings.

MacGillivray's Warbler

Geothlypis tolmiei

L 5″ | **WS** 7.5″

A shy and skulking warbler, usually difficult to see, but during the breeding season males perch on shrubs to perform their two-parted, low-pitched song. The MacGillivray's breeds in the north, the Coastal Ranges, the Sierra, and the mountains of the south, in low thickets in edge habitats near forest and water; it occurs as a migrant throughout the state. The second part of the throaty song is usually lower-pitched than the beginning, *chwee chwee chwee churr churr.* For some reason, radio commercials often have a MacGillivray's singing in the background. Call is a low, dry *chup*.

Large warbler with thick bill. Male gray-hooded, darker on mask and breast; white crescents around eyes. Green above and yellow below to under tail coverts.

Females and immatures duller. Gray-headed with whitish throat, white crescents around eyes. Green above and yellow below.

Common Yellowthroat

Geothlypis trichas

L 4.75" | **WS** 6.75"

The Yellowthroat is our only warbler that lives in cattail and tule marshes. It is found throughout the state, even in desert wetlands. The distinctively small, rather olive flanked birds of the Bay Area are known as the San Francisco Bay Common Yellowthroat; they sometimes breed in moist grassy areas with coyote brush, though they also nest in fresh or saltwater marshes. All yellowthroats are slim, with a rounded tail that is often cocked by excited birds. Females are confusingly much duller than males, but if a yellow bird comes out of a marsh, it is likely a yellowthroat. The song is a distinctive *whichichew whichichew whichichew*. The raspy call has a rubber-band quality, *phrrttt*.

Male has black mask with white fringe. Bright yellow throat and undertail coverts. Green above, no wing bars.

Female olive; dark sides of face contrast with bright yellow throat. Green-edged wing feathers, no wing bars.

Male vocalizes frequently during breeding season, often perching prominently; "pishing" noises by birders readily attract this warbler.

Yellow Warbler

Setophaga petechia

L 5" | **WS** 7"

Among the most widespread warblers, Yellow Warblers prefer open second-growth woods, such as riparian cottonwoods or willows. Yellow Warblers breed throughout California except in the desert; a small number winter in the extreme south. For unknown reasons, the species appears to be declining on the central coast and in some other areas, even where good habitat remains. There are still enough to our north that migrants are found all over the state, particularly in the fall. Autumn birds can be dull and not very yellowish, but they always show a thickset body, short tail, and a featureless face with a large dark eye. The pretty song is sometimes described as *sweet sweet I'm so sweet*; it is variable, but does tend to start with a repeated *tweet tweet* or *sweet sweet*. The call is a sharp *chip*.

Yellow warbler with short tail, beady black eye, and stout bill. Breeding male bright with rusty streaks below.

Short-tailed warbler. Females and immatures uniform yellow, dark beady eye, no strong face pattern.

Dull fall birds gray-toned; dull face with beady eye and dull eye ring. Short-tailed shape, yellow in tail.

Yellow-rumped Warbler

Setophaga coronata

L 5″ | **WS** 8.25″

Yellow-rumped Warblers are the hardiest of our warblers, wintering farther north than any other so long as food is available. When insects are not available, they resort to California wax myrtle and other berries. The two distinct populations in the US and Canada likely represent two different species. Birds of the western, "Audubon's Warbler" population breed in coniferous montane forests and winter widely in California. The more northern and eastern "Myrtle Warbler" is less common, wintering mainly at coastal sites, often in moister riparian vegetation than the Audubon's. The Audubon's song is a lazy warble, *seet seet seet seet sidle sidle,* usually dropping at the end. The Audubon's call is a low *tchip*; the Myrtle gives a lower, flatter *chep*.

Breeding male blue-gray above with yellow rump. Yellow throat bordered by blackish chest, yellow patches on breast sides. White panel on wing.

Fall birds duller; yellow throat, breast sides, and rump. Blue-gray face with crescents around eyes; washed brown above.

Some very dull and brownish, but rump always yellow. Yellow wash on throat; crescents around eye.

In the "Myrtle Warbler" of the boreal forest, male has white throat, dark mask, and pale eyebrow. Yellow rump and breast sides as "Audubon's," but less white on wing.

Townsend's Warbler

Setophaga townsendi

L 4.75" | **WS** 8"

The Townsend's replaces the very closely related Hermit Warbler as a breeder from central Oregon north. In California, the Townsend's is a migrant and wintering bird on the coastal slope, where it can be very common. It has a preference for coniferous trees, but is also found in deciduous woods, suburbs, parks, cemeteries, and riparian areas, often in mixed flocks with Yellow-rumped Warblers or chickadees in winter. It arrives in September and leaves by late May. Major springtime concentrations sometimes occur in desert oases such as Butterbredt Springs. The nasal, buzzy song tends to be two-parted, *bzz bzz bzz tzedle tzedle*. The call is a sharp *tsik*.

Male with black and yellow face; black mask with yellow teardrop. Black cap and throat. Green above with dark streaks; yellow breast and strongly streaked flanks. Tail with lots of white.

Female and immature duller; dark mask surrounded by yellow, yellow teardrop. Bold white wing bars; yellow below with streaking on breast and flanks.

Hermit Warbler

Setophaga occidentalis

L 5.5″ | **WS** 8″

A distinctive warbler with yellow head, black throat, and gray back, the Hermit breeds farther south than the very closely related Townsend's Warbler. Where the breeding ranges overlap in Oregon, they may hybridize, producing intermediate birds that are seen sometimes seen on migration through California. Hermit Warblers nest in northern California, the Sierra, the Coastal Ranges, and the higher elevations of the mountains of the south. A small number winter, mainly along the central coast. This species breeds in coniferous forests, but winterers and migrants can also be found in mixed forests. The song is higher-pitched and less buzzy than the Townsend's, and tends to end with an accented note *wizi wizi wizi wizi weezeee!* The call is a *tsik* like that of the Townsend's.

Adult male with yellow head and black throat. Gray above with dark streaks, two bold wing bars. White below, with no yellow. Tail white-edged in flight.

Female and immature duller; gray above with white wing bars, contrasting yellow face with isolated beady dark eye. Pale throat and underparts.

Black-throated Gray Warbler

Setophaga nigrescens

L 4.75" | **WS** 7.5"

This singular-looking warbler, gray, black, and white with a tiny yellow spot in front of the eye, breeds in California's oak forests, arid woodlands, and even tall chaparral. It breeds throughout the state in oak forest, and migrates through an even wider area. Spring migrants can be common at such desert "migrant traps" as Butterbredt Spring; the species winters south of California. The relatively buzzy song is more musical than that of the Townsend's Warbler, and often ends with an emphatic, higher-pitched note: *tzi tzi tzi tzi THEZEE*. Other songs can be very similar to the Hermit Warbler's. The call is lower and flatter than the Townsend's Warbler's *tchip*.

Adult male black and gray. Black crown, mask, and throat, with broad flaring eyebrow behind eye, odd little yellow spot before eye. Upperparts gray. Two white wing bars, white underparts with streaked flanks.

Female and immature duller; whitish throat, crown and mask dark gray rather than black. Yellow spot before eye obvious. Upperparts gray. Two white wing bars, white underparts with streaked flanks.

Wilson's Warbler

Cardellina pusilla

L 4.25" | **WS** 6"

A very cute-looking warbler with a large head and small bill, the Wilson's Warbler breeds in riparian and edge habitats with ample understory in the Coastal Ranges, in the north, and in the Sierra. Wilson's Warblers migrate through the entire state, from March to May in spring and in September and October in fall; they winter to the south of California. They keep low in the vegetation, often half-cocking the tail and slightly drooping the wings to create a distinctive silhouette. The song is a series of sharp, staccato notes, *chit chit chit chit chit chit*, sometimes with an emphasis on the last note. The call is a nasal *chimp*.

Active, often cocks tail. Male bright yellow with black beanie, face washed orange. Greenish above, no wing bars.

Large head and small bill. Female and immature with yellow eyebrow and darker cap. Green above, yellow below, no wing bars.

Yellow-breasted Chat

Icteria virens

L 7″ | **WS** 9.75″

Long considered a warbler, the Yellow-breasted Chat may be more properly placed in its own single-species family; the odd vocalizations, long rounded tail, large size, and thick, almost tanager-like bill are all unlike any other warbler's. Birds of dense riparian areas and other shrubby habitats, chats breed locally and uncommonly in California. They feed low, sometimes on the ground, but also have an aerial song display. Parts of the uniquely varied song recall blackbird calls, while the tempo and many repeated notes may remind one of a mockingbird song, with harsh notes and sweeter sounds mixed. The calls include a low *tuuk* and a sneezy *zcheew*.

Large, with thick bill, flat-topped head, and long tail. White eyebrow, lower eye crescent, and jaw stripe on gray face; greenish above, with lemon-yellow throat and breast.

Green-tailed Towhee

Pipilo chlorurus

L 7.25″ | **WS** 9.75″

Attractively dressed in gray and green, the small, slim Green-tailed Towhee breeds in shrubby areas at the edge of pine forest and in sagebrush thickets at lower elevations east of the Sierra. They move south to Mexico in winter. Like all towhees, it feeds on the ground but ascends to the top of a bush to sing . The loud, musical song is clearly punctuated, beginning with two exclamatory notes and closing with a varied phrase, *Chip-weeo, Teew Teew witchy!* The main calls are a cat-like *meeewww* and a high *pzip*.

Attractive, slim, and long-tailed. Largely gray, with green wings and tail and bright rusty cap. Bright white throat.

Spotted Towhee

Pipilo maculatus

L 7.5″ | **WS** 11″

Resident throughout California, except in the deserts of the southeast, this is a common bird of chaparral and shrubby edge; where the two overlap, the Spotted occupies moister habitats than the Green-tailed Towhee. Coastal and more northern populations of this species are darker, with less sexual dimorphism, while birds found east of the Sierra are paler and the females obviously browner. The song is a clipped note followed by a dull trill, *t'trrrrrrrrrrrrr.* The call is less cat-like and more nasal than that of the Green-tailed Towhee, *zhweeeewww.*

Male has black hood and red eye, obvious rusty flanks and vent. Black above, white spots on back, white wing bars. Long black tail with white corners in flight.

Female browner than male; red eyes, rusty flanks, spotted above.

California Towhee

Melozone crissalis

L 9″ | **WS** 11.5″

California Towhees are year-round residents of chaparral, and shrubby edge habitats west of the Sierra, commonly visiting backyard feeders. Strongly terrestrial, pairs may remain together for several years. The song, given more persistently in the evening than the morning, is a stuttering, accelerating series, *tic,tic,tic tititirrr*; the call is a sharp *chik!* Paired birds greet each other with a chattering duet.

Large, ground-loving songbird with long brownish tail. Brownish gray overall, with a rusty vent and rusty wash on face and throat. Crown warm brown.

Abert's Towhee

Melozone aberti

L 8.75" | **WS** 11"

The pale-billed, dark-faced Abert's entirely replaces the California Towhee in the southeastern desert, where it inhabits dense scrub, often near dry washes and moister areas. Individuals and pairs of this year-round, ground-dwelling resident are frequent visitors to feeders in towns. The two-part song accelerates in the second half, *tip-tip-tip-tip chichichrr*; it is higher-pitched, more strident, and less stuttering than that of California Towhee, with which the Abert's does not overlap in range. Calls a *seep* and a buzz.

Similar to California Towhee, but blackish face and upper throat. Averages paler, more grayish, with less-contrasting rusty vent.

Rufous-crowned Sparrow

Aimophila ruficeps

L 5.5" | **WS** 7.75"

The Rufous-crowned Sparrow likes grassy slopes with a few low shrubs and rocks to serve as song perches. As this species prefers drier habitats, south-facing slopes are more likely to be occupied, especially in the north of this sometimes shy and elusive bird's range; singing individuals are easier to see. Rufous-crowned Sparrows are resident on the coastal slope in the south, on the dry eastern slopes of the coastal mountains, and north along the foothills of the Sierra to approximately the latitude of Redding. The springy, musical song is a jumbled performance that incorporates the jumbled nature of a House Wren, and sweeter notes of a Lazuli Bunting. The alarm call is a nasal series, *few few few few few few.*

Grayish sparrow, unstreaked below. The black and white stripes below the cheek and the white eye ring draw attention to the face. Rufous crown, line behind eye, and streaking on gray back.

Chipping Sparrow

Spizella passerina

L 5.25" | **WS** 8.25"

A common migrant throughout California and winterer in the south, the Chipping Sparrow breeds in open woodlands or edge with a grassy understory; even very open habitats such as Christmas tree farms are used as long as there are a few trees or larger shrubs. Breeders occur in the north, the foothills of the Sierra, and the Coastal Ranges and on the southern coastal slope. Western Chipping Sparrows, including California's, migrate early in the fall beginning in late July during the desert monsoon, gathering in the desert to molt before continuing to the winter quarters. The song is a very dry, almost insect-like trill, drier and more mechanical-sounding than the trill of a junco. The call is a high *tsiip*.

Small, slim, and long-tailed. Breeding birds with rusty cap, white eyebrow, and black eye-line. Warm brown and streaked above, unstreaked below with white throat.

Nonbreeding birds with brownish streaked cap. Retains full dark eye line to base of bill.

Brewer's Sparrow

Spizella breweri

L 5.25" | **WS** 8"

Synonymous with Great Basin sagebrush flats with a grassy understory, the Brewer's Sparrow breeds east of the Sierra in California; migrants occur in the east and, in small numbers, on the coast in fall, and some winter in the desert of the southeast. Brewer's Sparrows form loose flocks in winter and migration; South Tufa in Mono Lake is a great place to see numbers in fall. The beautiful song is a long series of trills on changing pitches, many high-pitched but others low-pitched and harsh. The call is a high *tsiip*.

Small, slim, and long-tailed. Pale, with streaked upperparts. Weak face pattern with neat white eye ring, streaked crown.

Black-chinned Sparrow

Spizella atrogularis

L 5.5″ | **WS** 7.75″

This uncommon sparrow breeds in scattered localities on dry chaparral slopes in the Sierra Foothills, on the east side of the coastal mountains, and on the coastal slope of southern California. The northern limits of the range fluctuate from year to year depending on winter rainfall and habitat conditions farther south. They arrive in March and leave as early as late July, with a few remaining into October. The song is a very pleasing series of musical high-pitched notes that accelerate to a resonating trill. The call is a *tiip*.

Small, slim, long-tailed. Breeding male a beauty, gray with black face highlighting orange-pink bill. Rusty-brown upperparts with darker streaks.

Females, nonbreeders, and immatures similar to male but lack black face.

Vesper Sparrow

Pooecetes gramineus

L 5.75" | **WS** 9.5"

Large-headed and thickset, this oddly shaped sparrow breeds in agricultural fields, pastures, and sparse grassland with large areas of bare earth east of the Sierra; the preferred terrain is often flat, with some larger trees sometimes used as song perches. Vesper Sparrows migrate through most of the state and winter in the south. They have a complicated face pattern and a short tail with white outer feathers. The Vesper Sparrow's song begins with a repeated sweet whistled introductory note as in the Song Sparrow, but continues richer and lower-pitched. The call is a weak *tzip*.

Stocky, often looks front-heavy; short-tailed and thick-legged. Streaked breast. Complicated face pattern with white eye ring and dark cheek with paler center. Rusty shoulders; white outer tail feathers visible in flight.

Lark Sparrow

Chondestes grammacus

L 6.25″ | **WS** 11″

A strikingly patterned sparrow, with a complicated and attractive face pattern of white, rufous, and black, the Lark Sparrow is largely resident in California, where it is absent from the higher mountains and densely forested areas. This large, long-tailed species appears to require short grass with scattered large trees and patches of bare earth, a combination often found around ranch houses and pastures. When not breeding, loose flocks may use more shrubby habitats. Lark Sparrows have a very pleasant but disjointed song of trills and whistles, musical and varied with a springy quality. The call is a soft, high *tink*.

Harlequin face pattern, rusty white and black, white crescent below eye. Unstreaked below, black central breast spot. Brown above and streaked; rounded tail with white corners in flight.

Black-throated Sparrow

Amphispiza bilineata

L 5" | **WS** 8.5"

Once known as the "Desert Sparrow," this usually conspicuous species breeds in arid eastern areas of the state, inhabiting shrubby areas, ocotillo, and cacti adjacent to bare ground for feeding. It is particularly noticeable when singing. Found in California throughout the year, with an increase in numbers and a northward extension of the range from March to June. Juveniles are confusingly unlike adults; they lack the black throat, but show a bold white eyebrow and dark sides of the head, sharply demarcated from the white throat. The song is sweet and musical, the introductory notes followed by a liquid trill. Some birds sing a three-parted song. The call is a high, ringing *teep*.

Clean pattern. White eyebrow and malar stripe contrast with black face and throat. Unstreaked gray-brown above. Tail blackish with white tail corners.

Bell's Sparrow

Artemisiospiza belli

L 5.25" | **WS** 8.25"

The Bell's Sparrow is darker than the very similar and closely related Sagebrush Sparrow; it lacks streaks on the back and has a wider lateral throat stripe. The Bell's Sparrow is found west of the Sierra, not in sage habitats but in rabbitbrush and other coastal scrub and chaparral communities from central California to the Mexican border. The Carrizo Plain at Quail Springs is a great place to see this species, which is resident in California, with some dispersal in the late summer and fall. The rough-sounding warbling song does not exhibit much pitch change. The call is a high *tink*.

Gray-headed sparrow with short white stripe before eye; obvious white malar and wide dark stripe on side of throat. White below with central breast spot, buffy flanks. Unstreaked brownish gray back.

Savannah Sparrow

Passerculus sandwichensis

L 5" | **WS** 8.25"

This open-country bird happily does without trees at all, occupying agricultural land, pastures, beaches, and various other open habitats; some inhabit flat, open saltmarshes. California has three distinct populations of this species. The upland population breeds mainly in grasslands of the northern and central coast. The dark, heavily streaked "Belding's" Sparrow is resident in southern salt marshes. The "Large-billed" Sparrow, large, very pale above, and nearly unstreaked, arrives from Baja to winter at the Salton Sea, on southern coastal beaches, or in salt marshes. Each of these populations may represent a separate species. Savannah Sparrows have a high-pitched, buzzy, insect-like song that begins with a few short introductory notes, *tip tip tip tizTIZEEEEE tzup*. The call is a high *tsip*.

Small sparrow with contrasting breast streaking on white underparts. Face with yellow wash above eye, white mid-crown stripe. Streaked above, pinkish legs.

"Belding's" form of southern salt marshes darker, more heavily streaked below.

"Large-billed" form of Salton Sea and coastal sites in winter long-billed, pale, obscurely streaked above; no obvious yellow on face.

Grasshopper Sparrow

Ammodramus savannarum

L 4.5″ | **WS** 8″

Breeds in grasslands mainly throughout the state's coastal slope, and patchily in the Central Valley. A very small number remain in winter. The Grasshopper Sparrow occupies more arid, often older, and more varied grassland than the Savannah. If the grass is grazed or mowed too often, this sparrow will abandon the site. Juveniles are streaked on the breast, confusingly unlike the buffy, plain-breasted adults. Very secretive and usually difficult to see unless it is giving its very insect-like song, two dry introductory notes followed by a high buzz, *tik-tuk tziiiiiiiiiiiiii*; sometimes concludes with a high-pitched warbling. The call is a high *tiip*.

Large and flat-headed, with big bill, short tail, and long legs. Face warm buff with yellowish spot above eye and dark line behind eye; white mid-crown stripe. Yellow bend of wing often visible.

Lincoln's Sparrow

Melospiza lincolnii

L 5.5" | **WS** 7.75"

The shy Lincoln's Sparrow is less common and more colorful than the larger Song Sparrow. Narrowly streaked, with a peaked head and often surprised appearance, Lincoln's Sparrows tend to prefer deeper cover and moister areas than the Song; an inquisitive sparrow, it will readily come into view if you attract it by "pishing." A few Lincoln's breed in bogs in the Sierra, but this species is most often seen on migration and in winter. The seldom heard song is surprisingly rich and melodious. The calls include a high *tzip* and a buzzy *zeeep*.

Often looks surprised; can raise a crest. Gray wash on face, eye ring, warm brown tones above. Neat, narrow streaks below on buffy background.

Gray and warm brown on face; gray crown stripe and eyebrow. Fine narrow breast and flank streaks on buffy background, belly white.

Song Sparrow

Melospiza melodia

L 5.75″ | **WS** 8.25″

The well-known Song Sparrow is found throughout California, even in desert riparian areas. This species shows an incredible amount of geographic variation: dark and rufous in the northwest, heavily black-streaked in central California, paler eastwards, and pale rusty and gray in the desert. Three different forms, including the very large-billed birds of San Pablo Bay and Carquinez Strait, are restricted to saltmarsh habitats in the Bay Area; birds of these populations have evolved the ability to excrete salt to maintain their physiological salt balance, much like a marine bird. The rich, melodious song has three to five parts, beginning with short notes, *twi twi twi chup zleeeee zeet zeet*. The introductory notes are often described as *sweet sweet sweet*.... The distinctive call is a low *chimp*.

Longish, round-tipped tail. Gray and brown on face; pale malar with broad blackish stripe below it. Streaking below messy and blackish, coalesces into central spot. Wings and tail brown, back streaked.

Longish, round-tipped tail. Bold blackish brown lateral throat stripe bordered above by white malar. Streaking below can be blackish and dense, coalescing into central spot. Gray and brown, streaked above.

Dark rusty and gray Song Sparrows from the Pacific Northwest occur in winter.

Fox Sparrow

Passerella iliaca

L 7" | **WS** 10.25"

Fox Sparrows breed in brushy habitats at the edge of dry coniferous forests in the Sierra and southern mountains; they are widespread across California in winter and migration. Our breeding population, the "Thick-billed" Fox Sparrow, has a very big bill, gray head and back, sparse black streaking below, and rusty wings and tail; the high *teep* call is unlike that of the other forms. A dark brown form, the "Sooty" Fox Sparrow, occurs on the coastal slope in winter; these birds vary from dark brown to paler brown with some gray tones on the head, but all are densely streaked brown below, almost solid brown on the breast. A gray-headed version, the "Slate-colored" Fox Sparrow, with plumage like the Thick-billed, but a small bill and sharp *smack* call, like the Sooty, occurs in the south and deserts in winter. The song of the Fox Sparrow is a pleasant, melodious warbling.

Bulky sparrow with strong legs and largely yellow triangular bill. "Sooty" is unstreaked dark brownish gray above. Dark face, no stripes. Dense triangular streaking below coalesces into dark patch on breast.

"Thick-billed" has large beak. Paler than Sooty; gray head and back with rusty wings and tail. More sparsely marked below with blackish chevron or triangular shaped marks.

Some "Sooty" Fox Sparrows are chocolate-brown almost all over, densely streaked below with triangular marks. Large triangular bill with yellow base.

White-crowned Sparrow

Zonotrichia leucophrys

L 6" | **WS** 8.75"

Found throughout the state in winter, when it is common in shrubby edge habitats and backyards. The "Nuttall's" White-crowned is a resident breeder along the coast from central California north. The similar "Puget Sound" White-crowned arrives to winter, largely in coastal areas. The black-lored "Mountain" White-crowned breeds in shrubby edge habitats in the Sierra highlands, and occurs farther south in winter. The pink-billed, gray-plumaged "Gambel's" White-crowned of the boreal forest is found throughout the state in migration and winter. These forms are different enough that many individuals can be separated in the field; each has slightly different ecological requirements, making the White-crowned Sparrow one of the most interesting of California's backyard birds. The song varies between populations, but typically begins with one or two simple introductory whistles followed by buzzes or trills. The call is a sharp *pink*.

Adult with black and white head stripes, no streaking below. Coastal races have yellow bill with dark culmen, brown-washed back, buffy flanks and belly. Shorter wings than Gambel's.

Adult with black and white head stripes, no streaking below. "Gambel's" has pink-orange bill with small black tip, much gra wash on face and back.

Immatures like adults bu head stripes brown and buffy. Streaked above, unstreaked below with dull whitish wing bars, yellow to pinkish bill.

Golden-crowned Sparrow

Zonotrichia atricapilla

L 6.5" | **WS** 10"

A nonbreeding visitor to California from nesting grounds in Alaska and western Canada, the Golden-crowned sparrow winters in loose flocks mainly west of the Sierra and most commonly close to the coast. Winters in shrubby edge habitats, on average a little moister than those favored by the White-crowned, though the two are often found together. Backyards and feeders are a favored habitat. Arrives by early September, becomes common in October, and leaves in May. The amount of black retained on the crown of winter adults is proportional to their dominance in the flock. Late in winter they begin singing the simple whistled song, *Oh, dear meeee*. The call is a rising *pweew*.

A large, bulky sparrow. Breeding adult with black crown and yellow central crown stripe. Dark bill. Streaked brown and gray above, unstreaked grayish below.

Winter adults and immatures variably buffy to brownish below, streaked on upperparts. Dark bill. Black to brownish on crown, with more diffuse yellow patch on mid-crown, sometimes extending above eyes.

Dark-eyed Junco

Junco hyemalis

L 6" | **WS** 8.5"

Dark-eyed Juncos breed in dense conifers or eucalyptus with relatively open understory throughout California's mountains and other forested areas. While our populations are resident, migrants arrive from farther north in winter when these peculiar solid-colored sparrows with bright white outer tail feathers spread into parts of the state where they do not breed. A more uniformly gray form, the "Slate-colored" Junco, sometimes shows up in winter. The musical trilling song is much sweeter and more vibrant than the similar trill of the Chipping Sparrow. The call of the Dark-eyed Junco is a distinctive sharp *shup* that sounds almost as if it were being inhaled rather than exhaled.

Male strongly hooded, with pale pink bill. Rusty back, cinnamon flanks. In flight, dark tail with white sides.

Pink bill, white tail sides, hooded look, rusty back, cinnamon flanks. Female has grayish hood, sometimes washed brown.

Summer Tanager

Piranga rubra

L 6.75" | **WS** 12.25"

Summer Tanagers breed in riparian cottonwood forests in the foothills of the southern Sierra; a great place to find them is the Kern River Preserve. Migrants are occasionally found on the coast, but this species does not regularly winter in California. One of our few truly red birds, the adult male's bright plumage stands out strongly against green foliage; the female is a bit more subdued, but still lovely in her own right. The song is slower and slightly rougher than the similar song of the American Robin. The call is a *pit-tuk* or *pit-ti-chup*; a rattle is also heard.

Larger than warblers; thickset, with big thick bill. Male is all red.

Larger than warblers, with big thick bill. Female is yellowish all over, more grayish on upperparts.

Western Tanager

Piranga ludoviciana

L 7″ | **WS** 11.5″

California's most widespread tanager is quite common on migration throughout the state in edge habitats, forests, parks, oak woodlands, and willow thickets near streams. Western Tanagers breed in the mountains of the coast, the north, and the Sierra; they prefer to nest in coniferous forests, but can sometimes be found in deciduous woodland, keeping high in the canopy. Spring migration begins in April and peaks in early and mid-May; peak fall numbers occur from late August to mid-September, with most leaving by late October. The song is similar to that of an American Robin, but slower and very rough-sounding. The call is a rising *pi-di-dik*.

Breeding male yellow with red head and black back. Broad upper wing bar yellow, lower wing bar whitish; yellow rump.

Females and young variable yellowish below and on head, grayish above. Always show two wing bars, upper one more yellowish. Gray females have yellow undertail coverts.

Lazuli Bunting

Passerina amoena

L 5.5″ | **WS** 8.75″

Male Lazuli Buntings with their blue plumage and orange breast are superb; territorial males take exposed perches, where they are easy to see and enjoy in the edge habitats and shrubby sites near oak forests where they nest. Lazuli Buntings breed throughout California, except in the desert; their numbers vary from year to year, perhaps depending on winter rainfalls. Very widely distributed in migration, Lazuli Buntings arrive in April, with peak numbers in early May; good concentrations can be seen at such desert migrant traps as Butterbredt Springs. Fall migration peaks in September, with most birds gone by mid-October. The fast, melodious song usually has three parts, each with a different set of repeated notes. Gives a *pik* call note; migrants give a rough buzz in flight.

Finch-like bill. Gorgeous male with blue upperparts and head, rusty breast, and noticeably broad white upper wing bar. Superficially similar bluebirds have thin bills.

Female unstreaked brownish with finch-like bill. Two buffy wing bars; rump and tail may be washed dull blue.

Blue Grosbeak

Passerina caerulea

L 6″ | **WS** 11″

Larger and thicker-billed than the Lazuli Bunting, the Blue Grosbeak lives in edge habitats and weedy thickets adjacent to woods, where spring males sit out in the open as they sing. This is a breeding species in the southern half of the state, with some found farther north on the eastern rim of the Central Valley. Females have striking chestnut wing bars that distinguish them from buntings. All Blue Grosbeaks continually dip the tail. The song is a low-pitched warble with a pleasant cadence. The calls include a sharp *tink* and a buzzy flight call, harsher than the Lazuli Bunting's.

Thick bill; tail habitually flared and dipped. Male dark blue, with black before eyes and bold chestnut wing bars.

Thick bill; wags tail. Female buffy brown, with paler belly and chestnut wing bars.

Black-headed Grosbeak

Pheucticus melanocephalus

L 7.25" | **WS** 12.5"

Black-headed Grosbeaks breed in deciduous woodland, from cottonwoods to alder and willow, often preferring older groves. Breeding throughout California except in the desert, they arrive in April, with most gone south by mid-September; migrants are found anywhere in the state, often eating fruits and berries, especially in the fall. The song recalls that of an American Robin, but is faster, more hurried, and higher-pitched. The call is a sharp *pink*. The closely related Rose-breasted Grosbeak is a rare visitor, especially to the central coast; that species and the Black-headed Grosbeak are known to hybridize.

Thick bill. Male with black head contrasting with pumpkin-orange neck and underparts. Orange-striped black back, black wings marked with white. White wing patch and orange rump in flight.

Thick bill, round head. White eyebrow, darker crown and cheeks. Pumpkin-orange below, streaked brownish above, white wing bars.

Red-winged Blackbird

Agelaius phoeniceus

L 8″ | **WS** 14″

With their striking red shoulders, male Red-winged Blackbirds are one of the best-known and numerous of North American birds. These entertaining and fascinating birds tend to be polygynous, with each male mating with more than one female. Most of California's breeding Red-winged Blackbirds lack the yellow border to the shoulder. California females are very dark and closely resemble the females of the Tricolored, from which they cannot always be distinguished. The song is a gurgling and somewhat unattractive *gol-ga GLLEEERR*, the call a simple low *chuck*.

Black bird with red shoulders. Populations on coast and in Central Valley lack yellow fringe to the red "epaulet."

Blackish, pale throat and streaked below. Populations on coast and Central Valley very dark, solid blackish on lower breast and belly. Warm colored feather edges above.

Tricolored Blackbird

Agelaius tricolor

L 8" | **WS** 14"

Most of the world population of this singular species breeds in the Central Valley, with some on the central and southern coast. Tricolored Blackbirds breed in colonies sometimes numbering well into the thousands; almost all of the young in a given colony fledge at the same time. Sadly, this species is in a long-term decline, mainly as the result of habitat loss; a hundred years ago, some colonies contained tens or even hundreds of thousands of birds. The breeding colonies are in marshes or even blackberry thickets; they usually feed on fields and the edges of marshes. Large flocks frequent the coast in winter. The song and calls are more nasal than those of the Red-winged.

Slim, pointed bill. Male shiny black with dark red shoulder bordered below by white.

Female blackish brown with streaked breast. Slightly paler eyebrow. Edged with cold tones above, not rusty as in female Red-winged Blackbird.

Western Meadowlark

Sturnella neglecta

L 8.25″ | **WS** 16″

A widespread breeding bird in grassland and pastures, the Western Meadowlark is resident in California, with more on the coast and in the south in migration and winter. Winter flocks can include up to fifty birds, and may use more strictly agricultural habitats. Meadowlarks fly with an odd fluttering, often flaring the white outer tail feathers. The male sings from a prominent position on a shrub or fencepost. The song is loud and flute-like, whistled introductory notes followed by a rich, throaty flourish, *swee too-dlee WIDLE-DOO*. The calls include a short *chup* and a Hooded-Oriole-like *weeet*, often given in flight in winter.

Stocky, with long pinkish legs, long pointed bill. Yellow below with black V-shape on breast. Flanks spotted. Brownish above; white tail edges in flight.

Yellow-headed Blackbird

Xanthocephalus xanthocephalus

L 9.25" | **WS** 17"

The Yellow-headed Blackbird is a generally uncommon breeder in deep marshes, often tule marshes, in the Central Valley, east of the Sierra, and in the desert. Most leave California in winter, though numbers may remain at the Sacramento NWR; wintering flocks are often mixed with other blackbird species. This species has declined from its historical population numbers. The strongly polygynous males (mating with multiple females) spend much of their time singing their odd song from the top of emergent vegetation. Females are noticeably smaller; immature males, though similar to females in plumage, can often be sexed by their larger size. The main song is an ugly squawk with the quality of a rusty gate; another version of the song precedes the squawk with two introductory notes. The call is a rich *chuck*.

Large blackbird. Male black with yellow head and breast and neat black mask. In flight, white wing patches.

Female brownish black, with yellow breast; yellow wraps around a darker cheek patch.

Brewer's Blackbird

Euphagus cyanocephalus

L 9" | **WS** 14.5"

An incredibly adaptable and versatile species, the Brewer's Blackbird is a common resident throughout California in open habitats, including agriculture, grassland, and urban areas; when breeding in ornamental trees in towns, Brewer's Blackbirds may become aggressive, dive-bombing pedestrians that come too close. In parking lots and highway rest stops, they can be seen plucking dead insects from the grills of cars. The song is an odd explosive *ts-SCHLEEE*, accompanied by a fluffing of the plumage and flaring of the tail. The call is a flat *chet*.

Male black and shiny with "standard" tail. Bright yellow eye, purplish gloss on head, greenish blue gloss on body.

Female brownish gray with darker wings and tail, dark eyes, symmetrically proportioned bill.

Great-tailed Grackle

Quiscalus mexicanus

L 18″ | **WS** 22.75″

Great-tailed Grackles have been on a century-long march northward, each year colonizing a few more areas in California. They are fond of agricultural areas, golf courses, and even towns, but in the breeding season congregate in marshes with adjacent trees. They are still most common in the south, including the desert, but they are moving steadily north along the Central Coast and through the northern Central Valley. In winter, they may join mixed flocks with other blackbird species. The highly polygynous males defend a harem of females. Males are much larger than females; the size difference is among the largest in any bird species. The song is a complicated mix of trills, rattles, and loud whistles, given with cocked tail, drooped wings, and fluffed plumage. The call is a flat *chuk*.

Large, with long, keel-shaped tail and long, strong legs. Male shiny blackish with yellow eyes, blue body gloss, purplish head and neck.

Large blackbird with long, graduated tail. Female has yellow eyes; blackish above and warmer dull tawny below.

Brown-headed Cowbird

Molothrus ater

L 8" | **WS** 14"

Cowbirds are common residents throughout California in edge habitats, urban areas, and agricultural sites, where they actually perch on cattle, giving them their name. The only brood parasite among our common birds, the female cowbird lays her eggs in the nests of other species, such as vireos or warblers. The host parents feed and raise the cowbird young as their own, duped by their parental instincts; in the nests of smaller species, the cowbird young often outcompete the host's young, lowering their nesting success. The song of the Brown-headed Cowbird has the widest frequency range of any North American bird. It begins as a low liquid gurgling and rises into a high-pitched screech, *gluglug-shleee!* Females give a dry rattle; males have a whistled flight call.

Stocky blackbird with short bill, dark eyes. Male shiny black with brown head.

Small, stocky, and short-billed blackbird. Female brownish gray with dark eyes.

Scott's Oriole

Icterus parisorum

L 9" | **WS** 12.5"

This thickset, bulky oriole breeds in California's deserts, particularly at mid-elevations where there are junipers or oaks mixed with agaves and yuccas; it often suspends the hanging nest from such spiky plants as yuccas, Joshua trees, and Washingtonia fan palms. A few remain all year in southeastern California. The male's pleasant, flute-like song resembles that of the Western Meadowlark; the female sometimes sings a shorter, weaker version. Persistent singers, Scott's Orioles may continue into the heat of the day. The common calls include a harsh *chuck* and a scolding *cheh-cheh*.

Big oriole. Pointed bill with gray restricted to base of lower mandible. Male with yellow underparts and base of tail, black hood and wings, yellow shoulder.

Female brownish olive above, darker on throat, with dull yellow underparts. Two distinct white wing bars, hint of yellow shoulder.

Hooded Oriole

Icterus cucullatus

L 7.5″ | **WS** 10.5″

Mainly a breeding visitor, arriving in March and leaving by September, the Hooded Oriole has been spreading as we plant Washingtonia fan palms farther and farther north. Some remain all year in the south, where they can be found in native desert with fan palms. Hooded Orioles are very closely bound to the fan palm, hanging their basket nests from it and building the nest itself out of palm leaf fibers. Away from the deserts, they are urban and suburban birds in California. A nectar-feeder, this species commonly visits hummingbird feeders. The song is a choppy warble that sometimes resembles the song of a House Finch. The common call is a rising *wheet*; it also utters a chatter.

Slim oriole with thin, downcurved bill. Male orange-yellow on head, underparts, and rump. Black mask and throat, back, wings, and tail; broad white upper wing bar.

Slim oriole with thin, downcurved bill. Female grayish above, two wing bars, yellowish head and underparts.

Bullock's Oriole

Icterus bullockii

L 7" | **WS** 12"

Except for the desert, Bullock's Orioles breed throughout California in riparian forests, often of cottonwood or sycamore, often nesting in groups. The shallow hanging nest sometimes includes nylon fishing line if it is near lakes or creeks. Arrives from the south in April and May; males leave as early as mid-July, followed by the females in August. They molt in northern Mexico in the monsoon season before continuing south for the winter. The jovial whistled song has a slightly stuttering quality, *tchit-weeo teere chew chew*. The calls include a *tweeo* and a nasal rattle.

Short-tailed oriole with largely blue-gray bill. Male with orange head, underparts, and tail base. Head with black crown, eye-line, and throat. Large white panel on wing.

Female grayish with yellow-washed face, breast, and tail. Dark eye-line, orange eyebrow, two white wing bars.

Purple Finch

Haemorhous purpureus

L 5.5″ | **WS** 9.5″

Purple Finches are breeding residents in forests and at forest edges west of the Sierra crest; they commute to good feeding areas, including backyard feeders. Their abundance varies from year to year and season to season with changes in local food resources. Commonly confused with the House Finch, but male Purples are more reddish and differently shaped, larger with a larger bill, thick short legs, and a shorter tail. Female Purple Finches in California show only obscure streaking below. The lazy warbling song is much less energetic than the punctuated song of the House Finch. The flight call is a soft *piip*.

Male not purple, but strawberry all over, including back. Thick bill. Not obviously streaked.

Short tail, thick bill. Female brown and streaked, with paler eyebrow.

Cassin's Finch

Haemorhous cassinii

L 6.25" | **WS** 10.25"

The Cassin's Finch nests in dry conifer forests in the Sierra and the mountains of southern California; this species is resident in the state, but it moves downslope in winter. Particularly in the non-breeding season, it forms flocks of twenty or more, which may visit mountain bird feeders. Cassin's Finches are larger-billed, longer-winged, and more noticeably streaked on the back than Purples; the male Cassin's has a more clearly set-off red cap. The song is a loose warble, similar to a Purple Finch's but higher-pitched and faster. The flight call is a warbling *pidliip*.

Long, thick bill and long wings. Male pinkish red, brightest on crown. More streaked than Purple Finch.

Long, thick bill and long wings. Female more crisply and contrastingly streaked below than Purple; often crested.

House Finch

Haemorhous mexicanus

L 5.25″ | **WS** 8.75″

A highly successful and adaptable bird of edge habitats, the House Finch is now a common backyard bird even in urban areas, sometimes nesting right on houses. It feeds at bird feeders, in trees, or on the ground in weedy fields, retreating to higher vegetation when alarmed. The House Finch differs in color and pattern from the Purple Finch, and is longer-tailed and slimmer, with a shorter, more rounded bill. The House Finch's song is a lively warble, usually ending in a rougher, accented or upslurred note. The flight call is a liquid *pliip* or *veet*.

Smaller-billed and longer-tailed than Purple Finch. Male has broad red eyebrow, red throat and breast; back and wings brownish, flanks streaked.

Slim finch with long tail and rounded bill. Female is obscurely streaked below, dull face pattern.

Red Crossbill

Loxia curvirostra

L 6.75" | **WS** 10.25"

Red Crossbills are closely associated with conifers, where they extract seeds from the cones with their odd crossed bills. Some bills cross left, others right, allowing birds to feed from different sides of the same cones. Different populations of this species have different bill sizes and calls and songs; new species may be evolving as these populations adapt to specialize on certain tree species or cone sizes. Crossbills in the Sierra and Coastal Ranges are ponderosa pine specialists, while several different varieties occur in northwestern California. When their preferred seed crop fails, crossbills wander far and wide, ending up in areas where they do not regularly occur and eating foods they are not specialized for. The flight calls are sharp *jip!* or *kip!* notes.

Big-headed, short-tailed finch with unusual thick and cross-tipped bill. Male orange-red, with dark wings and notched tail.

Cross-tipped bill unique. Brownish female with greenish yellow crown and breast.

Pine Siskin

Spinus pinus

L 5″ | **WS** 8″

The Pine Siskin breeds in mixed forests in the north and Sierra, eating budding leaves and insects; it is a migrant or winter visitor to the rest of the state, all the way down to sea level on the central coast. They are fond of birch or alder seeds in winter, and move south in numbers when the northern food crop fails. Pine Siskins often call in flight, providing an easy way to detect them; they also visit backyard thistle feeders. The flight call is a *jee-it*; they also give a buzzy *zreee*. The song is a melodious jumble mixed with *zreee* notes.

Small finch with sharply pointed bill, short notched tail. Streaked above and below, with variable yellow edging on flight feathers and tail.

American Goldfinch

Spinus tristis

L 4.75″ | **WS** 8″

California is lucky to have three species of goldfinch. The American Goldfinch prefers more humid environments west of the Sierra, and is most common on the north and central coast. Some move south in winter. Unlike the other two species, the American tends to form single-species flocks. This is the largest goldfinch, and the only one with distinctly different breeding and non-breeding plumages. The typical undulating flight of goldfinches, up and down like a rollercoaster, seems to be most pronounced in the American. The song is a sweet jumbled warbling; the call note is often transcribed as *po-tato-chip*.

Small, with notched tail. Breeding male yellow with black crown and wings, pinkish bill.

Breeding female dull yellowish, with pinkish bill and greenish upperparts.

Non-breeding birds with tan back, yellowish face, buffy flanks, wing bars on dark wings.

Lesser Goldfinch

Spinus psaltria

L 4" | **WS** 7.75"

California's most widespread and commonly seen goldfinch, the Lesser Goldfinch is a bird of riparian thickets and the arid edges of oak and mixed woodlands, avoiding strictly coniferous forests. Resident throughout the state, though less common in the far north, this species is common at backyard feeders with thistle seed, often in small flocks and sometimes mixed with Lawrence's Goldfinches. The calls are mellow and somewhat sad-sounding, a downward *tweeew* and a nasal *cht-cht-cht*. The fast, varied song is peppered with *tweeew* notes and includes much mimicry, including rapid-fire imitations of Western Tanager calls, flicker vocalizations, Western Wood-Pewee songs, and, in urban settings, House Sparrow chirps.

Small finch with dark bill. Male green above with black cap and yellow underparts. White patch on wings.

Tiny, uniform finch with small bill. Greenish gray above, yellowish below, with dull whitish wing bars.

Lawrence's Goldfinch

Spinus lawrencei

L 4.25" | **WS** 8.25"

Resident in southern California but migratory in the north, this is an arid-country bird of the oak rim around the Central Valley and the foothills of the southern mountains. Small flocks, commonly joined by Lesser Goldfinches, occur in open oak and sycamore woodlands sometimes bordering chaparral slopes. The entire population is virtually limited to California, though birds periodically range east into Arizona. The calls are soft and bell-like, *tillup-tillup*. The song is slightly higher-pitched and faster than that of the Lesser Goldfinch; it includes mimicry and bell-like notes.

Small goldfinch. Male gray with black cap and face, yellow breast, and big yellow patches on wings.

Female a small gray goldfinch with bold yellow pattern on wings. Variable yellow wash on breast.

House Sparrow

Passer domesticus

L 6″ | **WS** 8.5″

One of the most familiar urban and suburban birds, the House Sparrow was introduced from Europe and is now a common backyard resident throughout California. Groups often visit feeders or "bathe" together in patches of dust. The bulky nest is often built in a hole or corner of a house or other building. The male often sings right above the nest. House Sparrows are continuous singers, stringing notes together into a seemingly endless, run-on series. The notes, each of which sounds like a simple call, are separated by a pause slightly longer than the note itself. The variable calls include a harsh, buzzy rattle and nasal raspings.

Stocky and thick-billed. Attractive male chestnut above, pale gray below. Gray crown, black and chestnut mask, pale cheeks, and black throat.

Stocky and thick-billed. Female drab brown, with pale brow behind eye, streaked back, buffy underparts.

Scaly-breasted Munia

Lonchura punctulata

L 4.5" | **WS** UNKNOWN

The Scaly-breasted Munia, introduced from Asia, is now common in southern California, particularly in the Los Angeles Basin and south to San Diego. A few are found in the Bay Area, in the South Bay, and in Sacramento, where the species does not seem to be firmly established yet. This little bird is light enough to perch on grass stalks and take seeds from the stem. Rather than eating seeds on the ground, they specialize in foraging for seeds while they are still on the grass stalks. These introduced populations favor feeders and grassy spots, including taller grass at the edge of parks, in urban areas. The songs are high-pitched and squeaky.

Tiny brownish bird with pointed tail and oversized blue-gray bill. Warm brown above, whitish below with bold dark scaling.

Author Acknowledgements

I am thankful that from my very first days in California, so many local birders helped me to learn about the birds of this amazingly diverse state. Joe Morlan took me out on my inaugural California birding trip to Mines Road, and once I moved to Half Moon Bay, those early years were spent motoring around California with Dave Powell. I am thankful to them, and to so many others who have shown me, taught me, and informed me, not only in the field, but also on e-mail lists and social media. Thanks to you all for the insights, and information, I am grateful.

The San Francisco Bay Bird Observatory has been instrumental in my learning about California birds, through research and bird banding there as a staff biologist, and more recently as an educator. I have been exposed to so much, and to so many great people that I can't emphasize the importance the organization has had on my growth. Sincerest thanks to all the bird clubs and Audubon Societies that have invited me to meet and talk to the birders, and see some local birds. Nothing is as invigorating and educational as talking with people about birds, in particular to beginning birders.

A special thanks to Rob Fowler for filling me in on some northwestern California birding sites and information. George Scott and Charles Nix have been a delight to work with, making this large project easy and smooth for me. Finally, none of this would have been possible were it not for the immense patience and understanding from my family. Katja, Pablo, Bianca (and Riley, Ruby, Olivia, Pumpkin, Spots, and Oreo too), I love you all and thanks for letting me be the birdwatcher dad.

—Alvaro Jaramillo,
Half Moon Bay, California,
April 2015

Scott & Nix Acknowledgments

Many thanks to Alvaro Jaramillo, and to Jeffrey A. Gordon, Louis Morrell, and everyone at the American Birding Association for their good work. Special thanks to Curt Matthews at Independent Book Publishers (IPG) along with his colleagues, Mark Voigt, Mark Noble, Jeff Palicki, Michael Riley, Mary Knowles, Cynthia Murphy, and many others. Thanks to Alan Poole, Miyoko Chu, and especially Kevin J. McGowan at the Cornell Lab of Ornithology. We give special thanks to Brian E. Small for his extraordinary photography and to all the others whose images illuminate this guide, including Mike Danzenbaker, Bob Steele, Alan Murphy, Jim Zipp, and the photographers represented by VIREO (Visual Resources for Ornithology). We thank Rick Wright and Paul Hess for their excellent work on the manuscript; James Montalbano of Terminal Design for his typefaces; and René Nedelkoff of Four Colour Print Group for shepherding this book through print production.

Image Credits

(T) = Top, (B) = Bottom, (L) = Left, (R) = Right, (M) = Middle, (TL) = Top left, (TR) = Top right, (BL) = Bottom left, (BR) = Bottom right; pages with multiple images from one source are indicated by a single credit.

XIII–XXIX Brian E. Small. **XXV** Mike Danzenbaker. **XXVI–XXXVII** Brian E. Small. **2** Brian E. Small. **3** Brian E. Small. **4** Brian E. Small. **5** Brian E. Small. **6** Brian E. Small. **7** Brian E. Small. **8** Brian E. Small. **9** Brian E. Small. **10** Brian E. Small. **11** Brian E. Small. **12** Brian E. Small. **13** Brian E. Small (T). Mike Danzenbaker (B). **14** Brian E. Small. **15** Brian E. Small (T). Mike Danzenbaker (B). **16** Brian E. Small. **17** Brian E. Small. **18** Brian E. Small. **19** Brian E. Small. **20** Brian E. Small. **21** Brian E. Small (T). Mike Danzenbaker (B). **22** Brian E. Small. **23** Brian E. Small. **24** Brian E. Small. **25** Brian E. Small. **26** Brian E. Small. **27** Brian E. Small. **28** Mike Danzenbaker (T). Jim Zipp (B). **29** Brian E. Small. **30** Brian E. Small. **31** Brian E. Small. **32** Brian E. Small. **33** Brian E. Small. **34** Brian E. Small. **35** Brian E. Small. **36** Brian E. Small. **37** Brian E. Small. **38** Brian E. Small. **39** Alan Murphy **40** Brian E. Small. **41** Brian E. Small (T). Bob Steele (B). **42** Brian E. Small. **43** Brian E. Small. **44** Brian E. Small. **45** Brian E. Small. **46** Brian E. Small. **47** Brian E. Small. **48** Brian E. Small. **49** Brian E. Small. **50** Brian E. Small. **51** Brian E. Small. **52** Brian E. Small. **53** Mike Danzenbaker (T). Alan Murphy (B). **54** Alan Murphy (T). Mike Danzenbaker (B). **55** Brian E. Small. **56** Brian E. Small. **57** Brian E. Small. **58** Brian E. Small. **59** Brian E. Small. **60** Brian E. Small. **61** Brian E. Small. **62** Brian E. Small. **63** Brian E. Small. **64** Brian E. Small. **65** Brian E. Small. **66** Brian E. Small. **67** Brian E. Small. **68** Brian E. Small. **69** Brian E. Small. **70** Brian E. Small. **71** Brian E. Small. **72** C. Van Cleve/VIREO. **73** G. Bartley/VIREO (T). Brian E. Small. **74** Brian E. Small. **75** Brian E. Small (T). Alan Murphy (B). **76** Brian E. Small. **77** Brian E. Small. **78** Brian E. Small (T). Alan Murphy (B). **79** Brian E. Small (T). Mike Danzenbaker (B). **80** Brian E. Small. **81** Bob Steele. **82** Mike Danzenbaker. **83** Brian E. Small (T). Mike Danzenbaker (M). Mike Danzenbaker (B). **84** Brian E. Small (T). Alan Murphy (B). **85** Brian E. Small (T). Bob Steele (B). **86** Brian E. Small. **87** Brian E. Small. **88** Brian E. Small. **89** Brian E. Small. **90** Brian E. Small. **91** Brian E. Small. **92** Brian E. Small. **93** Brian E. Small. **94** Brian E. Small. **95** Brian E. Small (TL). Brian E. Small (TR). Mike Danzenbaker (B). **96** Brian E. Small. **97** Brian E. Small. **98** Brian E. Small. **99** Brian E. Small. **100** Brian E. Small. **101** Brian E. Small. **102** Brian E. Small. **103** Brian E. Small (T). Mike Danzenbaker (B). **104** Brian E. Small. **105** Brian E. Small. **106** Brian E. Small. **107** Brian E. Small. **108** Brian E. Small. **109** Brian E. Small. **110** Brian E. Small. **111** Brian E. Small. **112** Brian E. Small. **113** Brian E. Small. **114** Brian E. Small. **115** Brian E. Small. **116** Brian E. Small. **117** Brian E. Small. **118** Brian E. Small. **119** Brian E. Small. **120** Brian E. Small. **121** Brian E. Small. **122** Brian E. Small. **123** Brian E. Small. **124** Alan Murphy **125** Mike Danzenbaker (T). Brian E. Small (B). **126** Mike Danzenbaker (T). Brian E. Small (B). **127** Mike Danzenbaker. **128** Mike Danzenbaker. **129** Mike Danzenbaker. **130** Alvaro Jaramillo. **131** Mike Danzenbaker. **132** Brian E. Small (L). Alan Murphy (R). **133** Brian E. Small. **134** Brian E. Small (T). Bob Steele (B). **135** Mike Danzenbaker. **136** Brian E. Small (T). Bob Steele (B). **137** Brian E. Small. **138** Brian E. Small. **139** Brian E. Small (T). Bob Steele (B). **140** Bob Steele. **141** Alvaro Jaramillo (T). Brian E. Small (B). **142** Bob Steele. **143** Alan Murphy (T). Bob Steele (B). **144** Brian E. Small (T). Alvaro Jaramillo (B). **145** Brian E. Small. **146** Brian E. Small (T). Alan Murphy (B). **147** Brian E. Small. **148** Brian E. Small. **149** Brian E. Small. **150** Brian E. Small. **151** Brian E. Small. **152** Brian E. Small. **153** Brian E. Small. **154** Brian E. Small. **155** Brian E. Small. **156** Brian E. Small. **157** Alan Murphy. **158** Brian E. Small. **159** Brian E. Small. **160** Bob Steele. **161** Brian E. Small. **162** Brian E. Small. **163** Brian E. Small. **164** Brian E. Small. **165** Brian E. Small. **166** Brian E. Small. **167** Brian E. Small. **168** Brian E. Small. **169** Brian E. Small (T). Bob Steele (B). **170** Brian E. Small. **171** Mike Danzenbaker (T). S. Mlodinow/VIREO (B). **172** Mike Danzenbaker. **173** Brian E. Small. **174** Brian E. Small. **175** Brian E. Small. **176** Brian E. Small (T). Alan Murphy (B). **177** Brian E. Small. **178** Brian E. Small (T). Alan Murphy (B). **179** Brian E. Small. **180** Brian E. Small. **181** Brian E. Small. **182** Brian E. Small. **183** Brian E. Small. **184** Brian E. Small. **185** Brian E. Small. **186** Brian E. Small. **187** Brian E. Small. **188** Brian E. Small. **189** Brian E. Small. **190** Brian E. Small. **191** Brian E. Small. **192** Brian E. Small. **193** Brian E. Small (T). Jim Zipp (B). **194** Mike Danzenbaker (T). Alan Murphy (B). **195** Bob Steele (T). Brian E. Small (B). **196** Brian E. Small (T). Bob Steele (B). **197** Brian E. Small. **198** Brian E. Small. **199** Brian E. Small. **200** Brian E. Small. **201** Brian E. Small. **202** Brian E. Small. **203** Brian E. Small. **204** Brian E. Small. **205** Brian E. Small. **206** Brian E. Small. **207** Brian E. Small. **208** Brian E. Small. **209** Brian E. Small. **210** Brian E. Small. **211** Brian E. Small. **212** Brian E. Small. **213** Brian E. Small. **214** Brian E. Small. **215** Brian E. Small. **216** Brian E. Small. **217** Brian E. Small. **218** Brian E. Small. **219** Brian E. Small. **220** Brian E. Small. **221** Brian E. Small. **222** Brian E. Small.

223 Brian E. Small. **224** Brian E. Small (L). R. Curtis/VIREO (R). **225** Brian E. Small (L). Bob Steele (R). **226** Mike Danzenbaker. **227** Brian E. Small (L). Bob Steele (R). **228** A. Morris/VIREO (L). Bob Steele (R). **229** Brian E. Small (L). Mike Danzenbaker (R). **230** Brian E. Small (T). Bob Steele (B). **231** Brian E. Small. **232** Brian E. Small. **233** Brian E. Small. **234** Brian E. Small. **235** Brian E. Small. **236** Brian E. Small. **237** Brian E. Small. **238** Brian E. Small. **239** Brian E. Small. **240** Brian E. Small. **241** Brian E. Small. **242** Brian E. Small. **243** Brian E. Small. **244** Brian E. Small. **245** Brian E. Small. **246** Brian E. Small. **247** Brian E. Small. **248** Brian E. Small. **249** Brian E. Small. **250** Brian E. Small. **251** Brian E. Small. **252** Brian E. Small. **253** Brian E. Small. **254** Brian E. Small. **255** Brian E. Small. **256** Brian E. Small. **257** Brian E. Small. **258** Brian E. Small. **259** Brian E. Small. **260** Brian E. Small. **261** Brian E. Small. **262** Brian E. Small. **263** Brian E. Small. **264** Brian E. Small. **265** Brian E. Small. **266** Brian E. Small. **267** Brian E. Small. **268** Brian E. Small. **269** Brian E. Small. **270** Brian E. Small. **271** Brian E. Small. **272** Brian E. Small. **273** Brian E. Small. **273** Brian E. Small. **274** Brian E. Small. **275** Brian E. Small. **276** Brian E. Small. **277** Brian E. Small. **278** Brian E. Small. **279** Brian E. Small. **280** Brian E. Small. **281** Brian E. Small. **282** Brian E. Small. **283** Brian E. Small. **284** Brian E. Small. **285** Brian E. Small. **286** Brian E. Small. **287** Brian E. Small. **288** Brian E. Small. **289** Brian E. Small. **290** Brian E. Small. **291** Brian E. Small. **292** Brian E. Small. **293** Brian E. Small. **294** Brian E. Small. **295** Brian E. Small. **296** Brian E. Small. **297** Brian E. Small. **298** Brian E. Small. **299** Brian E. Small. **300** Brian E. Small. **301** Brian E. Small. **302** Brian E. Small. **303** Brian E. Small. **303** Brian E. Small. **304** Brian E. Small. **305** Brian E. Small. **306** Brian E. Small. **307** Brian E. Small. **308** Alan Murphy (TL). Brian E. Small (TR). Brian E. Small (B). **309** Brian E. Small. **310** Brian E. Small. **311** Brian E. Small. **312** Brian E. Small. **313** Brian E. Small. **314** Brian E. Small. **315** Brian E. Small. **316** P. LaTourrette/VIREO (L). Brian E. Small (R). **317** Brian E. Small. **318** Brian E. Small. **319** Brian E. Small. **320** Brian E. Small. **321** Brian E. Small (T). Bob Steele (B). **322** Brian E. Small. **323** Brian E. Small. **324** Brian E. Small. **325** Brian E. Small. **326** Bob Steele (T). Brian E. Small (B). **327** Brian E. Small. **328** Brian E. Small. **329** Brian E. Small. **330** Brian E. Small. **331** Brian E. Small. **332** Brian E. Small. **333** Brian E. Small. **334** Brian E. Small. **335** M. Hale/VIREO.

Official California Checklist by the California Bird Records Committee

The sequence of birds on this list has been updated to follow the 7th edition of the *A.O.U Check-List of North American Birds*, and supplements.

A total of 659 species is included on this official California checklist, 11 of which are established introductions, one of which has been extirpated within historical times, and one of which is in the process of being reintroduced but is not yet established. An additional five species have been recorded in the state, but are of uncertain natural occurrence and are included in a supplemental list following the main list.

For new species to be added to the main list, at least one record of the species must be reviewed and accepted by the California Bird Records Committee (CBRC). All species on this list except those annotated with P, V, A or S are supported by at least one extant specimen obtained in California. Species not supported by specimens are documented either by photographs (P), video recordings (V), audio recordings (A), or sight records (S) with one or more convincing written descriptions, but no other tangible evidence. Documentation supporting all records reviewed by the CBRC (except for the physical specimens) is permanently archived at the Western Foundation of Vertebrate Zoology, 439 Calle San Pablo, Camarillo, California 93012-8506, where it is available to researchers.

The CBRC solicits documentation for all occurrences in California of species on its Review List (those annotated below with an asterisk), as well as species not yet recorded in California. In general, review species average four or fewer occurrences per year in California over the most recent ten year period. Documentation should be sent to Guy McCaskie, California Bird Records Committee, by e-mail to secretary@californiabirds.org. We also seek documentation concerning the potential establishment of introduced species not currently on the state list.

Updated 26 January 2015. Retrieved from www.californiabirds.org/ca_list.asp

Legend

- * California Bird Records Committee Review Species (189 species)
- I Introduced but now established in California (11 species)
- E Extirpated from California (1 species)
- RI Reintroduction in progress—not yet established. (1 species)

For species not supported by curated specimens (116 species):

- P At least one record supported by identifiable photograph (114 species)
- V At least one record supported by identifiable video (24 species)
- A At least one record supported by identifiable audio recording (9 species)
- S Supported only by sight records (2 species)

Ducks, Geese, and Swans

☐ Black-bellied Whistling-Duck *P
☐ Fulvous Whistling-Duck *
☐ Tundra Bean-Goose *P
☐ Greater White-fronted Goose
☐ Emperor Goose *
☐ Snow Goose
☐ Ross's Goose
☐ Brant
☐ Cackling Goose
☐ Canada Goose
☐ Trumpeter Swan P
☐ Tundra Swan
☐ Whooper Swan *P
☐ Wood Duck
☐ Gadwall
☐ Falcated Duck *P
☐ Eurasian Wigeon
☐ American Wigeon
☐ American Black Duck *
☐ Mallard
☐ Blue-winged Teal
☐ Cinnamon Teal
☐ Northern Shoveler
☐ Northern Pintail
☐ Garganey *
☐ Baikal Teal *
☐ Green-winged Teal
☐ Canvasback
☐ Redhead
☐ Common Pochard *P
☐ Ring-necked Duck
☐ Tufted Duck
☐ Greater Scaup
☐ Lesser Scaup
☐ Steller's Eider *P
☐ King Eider *
☐ Common Eider *P
☐ Harlequin Duck
☐ Surf Scoter
☐ White-winged Scoter
☐ Black Scoter
☐ Long-tailed Duck
☐ Bufflehead
☐ Common Goldeneye
☐ Barrow's Goldeneye
☐ Smew *PV
☐ Hooded Merganser
☐ Common Merganser
☐ Red-breasted Merganser
☐ Ruddy Duck

New World Quail

☐ Mountain Quail
☐ California Quail
☐ Gambel's Quail

Partridges, Grouse, Turkeys, and Old World Quail

☐ Chukar I
☐ Ring-necked Pheasant I
☐ Ruffed Grouse
☐ Greater Sage-Grouse
☐ White-tailed Ptarmigan IP
☐ Sooty Grouse
☐ Sharp-tailed Grouse E
☐ Wild Turkey I

Loons

☐ Red-throated Loon
☐ Arctic Loon *
☐ Pacific Loon
☐ Common Loon
☐ Yellow-billed Loon *

Grebes

☐ Least Grebe *
☐ Pied-billed Grebe
☐ Horned Grebe
☐ Red-necked Grebe
☐ Eared Grebe
☐ Western Grebe
☐ Clark's Grebe

Albatrosses

☐ White-capped Albatross *P
☐ Salvin's Albatross *P
☐ Light-mantled Albatross *PV
☐ Wandering Albatross *P
☐ Laysan Albatross
☐ Black-footed Albatross
☐ Short-tailed Albatross *

Shearwaters and Petrels

☐ Northern Fulmar
☐ Great-winged Petrel *PV
☐ Murphy's Petrel
☐ Mottled Petrel
☐ Hawaiian Petrel PV
☐ Cook's Petrel
☐ Stejneger's Petrel *P
☐ Bulwer's Petrel *P
☐ White-chinned Petrel *PV
☐ Parkinson's Petrel *P
☐ Streaked Shearwater *
☐ Cory's Shearwater *P
☐ Pink-footed Shearwater
☐ Flesh-footed Shearwater
☐ Great Shearwater *P
☐ Wedge-tailed Shearwater *P
☐ Buller's Shearwater
☐ Sooty Shearwater

- ☐ Short-tailed Shearwater
- ☐ Manx Shearwater PV
- ☐ Townsend's Shearwater *
- ☐ Black-vented Shearwater

Storm-Petrels

- ☐ Wilson's Storm-Petrel
- ☐ Fork-tailed Storm-Petrel
- ☐ Ringed Storm-Petrel *P
- ☐ Leach's Storm-Petrel
- ☐ Ashy Storm-Petrel
- ☐ Wedge-rumped Storm-Petrel *
- ☐ Black Storm-Petrel
- ☐ Tristram's Storm-Petrel *P
- ☐ Least Storm-Petrel

Tropicbirds

- ☐ White-tailed Tropicbird *P
- ☐ Red-billed Tropicbird
- ☐ Red-tailed Tropicbird *

Storks

- ☐ Wood Stork

Frigatebirds

- ☐ Magnificent Frigatebird *
- ☐ Great Frigatebird *P
- ☐ Lesser Frigatebird *P

Boobies and Gannets

- ☐ Masked Booby *P
- ☐ Nazca Booby *P
- ☐ Blue-footed Booby
- ☐ Brown Booby
- ☐ Red-footed Booby *
- ☐ Northern Gannet *P

Cormorants

- ☐ Brandt's Cormorant
- ☐ Neotropic Cormorant P
- ☐ Double-crested Cormorant
- ☐ Pelagic Cormorant

Darters

- ☐ Anhinga *P

Pelicans

- ☐ American White Pelican
- ☐ Brown Pelican

Herons, Bitterns, and Allies

- ☐ American Bittern
- ☐ Least Bittern
- ☐ Great Blue Heron
- ☐ Great Egret
- ☐ Snowy Egret
- ☐ Little Blue Heron
- ☐ Tricolored Heron *
- ☐ Reddish Egret
- ☐ Cattle Egret
- ☐ Green Heron
- ☐ Black-crowned Night-Heron
- ☐ Yellow-crowned Night-Heron

Ibises and Spoonbills

- ☐ White Ibis *
- ☐ Glossy Ibis *P
- ☐ White-faced Ibis
- ☐ Roseate Spoonbill *

New World Vultures

- ☐ Black Vulture *P
- ☐ Turkey Vulture
- ☐ California Condor RI

Ospreys

- ☐ Osprey

Hawks, Kites, Eagles, and Allies

- ☐ Swallow-tailed Kite *P
- ☐ White-tailed Kite
- ☐ Mississippi Kite *
- ☐ Bald Eagle
- ☐ Northern Harrier
- ☐ Sharp-shinned Hawk
- ☐ Cooper's Hawk
- ☐ Northern Goshawk
- ☐ Common Black Hawk *P
- ☐ Harris's Hawk
- ☐ Red-shouldered Hawk
- ☐ Broad-winged Hawk
- ☐ Gray Hawk *PV
- ☐ Swainson's Hawk
- ☐ Zone-tailed Hawk
- ☐ Red-tailed Hawk
- ☐ Ferruginous Hawk
- ☐ Rough-legged Hawk
- ☐ Golden Eagle

Rails, Gallinules, and Coots

- ☐ Yellow Rail
- ☐ Black Rail
- ☐ Ridgway's Rail
- ☐ Virginia Rail
- ☐ Sora
- ☐ Purple Gallinule *
- ☐ Common Gallinule
- ☐ American Coot

Cranes

- ☐ Sandhill Crane
- ☐ Common Crane *P

Stilts and Avocets

- ☐ Black-necked Stilt
- ☐ American Avocet

Oystercatchers

- ☐ American Oystercatcher
- ☐ Black Oystercatcher

Lapwings and Plovers

- ☐ Black-bellied Plover
- ☐ American Golden-Plover
- ☐ Pacific Golden-Plover
- ☐ Lesser Sand-Plover *P
- ☐ Greater Sand-Plover *PV
- ☐ Snowy Plover
- ☐ Wilson's Plover *
- ☐ Common Ringed Plover *PVA
- ☐ Semipalmated Plover
- ☐ Piping Plover *P
- ☐ Killdeer
- ☐ Mountain Plover
- ☐ Eurasian Dotterel *PV

Sandpipers, Phalaropes, and Allies

- ☐ Terek Sandpiper *PV
- ☐ Spotted Sandpiper
- ☐ Solitary Sandpiper
- ☐ Gray-tailed Tattler *P
- ☐ Wandering Tattler
- ☐ Spotted Redshank *P
- ☐ Greater Yellowlegs
- ☐ Common Greenshank *PV
- ☐ Willet
- ☐ Lesser Yellowlegs
- ☐ Marsh Sandpiper *P

- ☐ Wood Sandpiper *P
- ☐ Upland Sandpiper *
- ☐ Little Curlew *P
- ☐ Whimbrel
- ☐ Bristle-thighed Curlew *PV
- ☐ Long-billed Curlew
- ☐ Hudsonian Godwit *P
- ☐ Bar-tailed Godwit *
- ☐ Marbled Godwit
- ☐ Ruddy Turnstone
- ☐ Black Turnstone
- ☐ Red Knot
- ☐ Surfbird
- ☐ Ruff
- ☐ Sharp-tailed Sandpiper
- ☐ Stilt Sandpiper
- ☐ Curlew Sandpiper *
- ☐ Long-toed Stint *P
- ☐ Red-necked Stint *P
- ☐ Sanderling
- ☐ Dunlin
- ☐ Rock Sandpiper
- ☐ Baird's Sandpiper
- ☐ Little Stint *
- ☐ Least Sandpiper
- ☐ White-rumped Sandpiper *
- ☐ Buff-breasted Sandpiper
- ☐ Pectoral Sandpiper
- ☐ Semipalmated Sandpiper
- ☐ Western Sandpiper
- ☐ Short-billed Dowitcher
- ☐ Long-billed Dowitcher
- ☐ Jack Snipe *
- ☐ Wilson's Snipe
- ☐ Common Snipe *P
- ☐ American Woodcock *P
- ☐ Wilson's Phalarope
- ☐ Red-necked Phalarope
- ☐ Red Phalarope

Skuas

- ☐ South Polar Skua
- ☐ Pomarine Jaeger
- ☐ Parasitic Jaeger
- ☐ Long-tailed Jaeger

Auks, Murres, and Puffins

- ☐ Common Murre
- ☐ Thick-billed Murre *
- ☐ Pigeon Guillemot
- ☐ Long-billed Murrelet *
- ☐ Marbled Murrelet
- ☐ Kittlitz's Murrelet *
- ☐ Scripps's Murrelet
- ☐ Guadalupe Murrelet
- ☐ Craveri's Murrelet
- ☐ Ancient Murrelet
- ☐ Cassin's Auklet
- ☐ Parakeet Auklet
- ☐ Least Auklet *
- ☐ Crested Auklet *
- ☐ Rhinoceros Auklet
- ☐ Horned Puffin
- ☐ Tufted Puffin

Gulls, Terns, and Skimmers

- ☐ Swallow-tailed Gull *P
- ☐ Black-legged Kittiwake
- ☐ Red-legged Kittiwake *
- ☐ Ivory Gull *P
- ☐ Sabine's Gull
- ☐ Bonaparte's Gull
- ☐ Black-headed Gull *P
- ☐ Little Gull *
- ☐ Ross's Gull *P
- ☐ Laughing Gull
- ☐ Franklin's Gull
- ☐ Belcher's Gull *PV
- ☐ Black-tailed Gull *
- ☐ Heermann's Gull
- ☐ Mew Gull
- ☐ Ring-billed Gull
- ☐ Western Gull
- ☐ Yellow-footed Gull
- ☐ California Gull
- ☐ Herring Gull
- ☐ Thayer's Gull
- ☐ Iceland Gull *P
- ☐ Lesser Black-backed Gull
- ☐ Slaty-backed Gull *P
- ☐ Glaucous-winged Gull
- ☐ Glaucous Gull
- ☐ Great Black-backed Gull *P
- ☐ Sooty Tern *
- ☐ Bridled Tern *P
- ☐ Least Tern
- ☐ Gull-billed Tern
- ☐ Caspian Tern
- ☐ Black Tern
- ☐ White-winged Tern *PV
- ☐ Common Tern
- ☐ Arctic Tern
- ☐ Forster's Tern
- ☐ Royal Tern
- ☐ Sandwich Tern *P
- ☐ Elegant Tern
- ☐ Black Skimmer

Pigeons and Doves

- ☐ Rock Pigeon I
- ☐ Band-tailed Pigeon
- ☐ Oriental Turtle-Dove *PV
- ☐ Eurasian Collared-Dove I
- ☐ Spotted Dove I
- ☐ Inca Dove
- ☐ Common Ground-Dove
- ☐ Ruddy Ground-Dove
- ☐ White-winged Dove
- ☐ Mourning Dove

Cuckoos, Roadrunners, and Anis

- ☐ Common Cuckoo *PV
- ☐ Yellow-billed Cuckoo
- ☐ Black-billed Cuckoo *
- ☐ Greater Roadrunner
- ☐ Groove-billed Ani *P

Barn Owls

- ☐ Barn Owl

Typical Owls

- ☐ Flammulated Owl
- ☐ Western Screech-Owl
- ☐ Great Horned Owl
- ☐ Snowy Owl *
- ☐ Northern Pygmy-Owl
- ☐ Elf Owl *
- ☐ Burrowing Owl
- ☐ Spotted Owl
- ☐ Barred Owl
- ☐ Great Gray Owl
- ☐ Long-eared Owl
- ☐ Short-eared Owl
- ☐ Northern Saw-whet Owl

Goatsuckers

- ☐ Lesser Nighthawk
- ☐ Common Nighthawk
- ☐ Common Poorwill
- ☐ Chuck-will's-widow *
- ☐ Buff-collared Nightjar *
- ☐ Eastern Whip-poor-will *PA
- ☐ Mexican Whip-poor-will

Swifts

- ☐ Black Swift
- ☐ White-collared Swift *S
- ☐ Chimney Swift
- ☐ Vaux's Swift
- ☐ Common Swift *P
- ☐ White-throated Swift

Hummingbirds

- ☐ Green Violetear *P
- ☐ Magnificent Hummingbird *P
- ☐ Blue-throated Hummingbird *P
- ☐ Ruby-throated Hummingbird *
- ☐ Black-chinned Hummingbird
- ☐ Anna's Hummingbird
- ☐ Costa's Hummingbird
- ☐ Broad-tailed Hummingbird
- ☐ Rufous Hummingbird
- ☐ Allen's Hummingbird
- ☐ Calliope Hummingbird
- ☐ Broad-billed Hummingbird *P
- ☐ Violet-crowned Hummingbird *P
- ☐ Xantus's Hummingbird *P

Kingfishers

- ☐ Belted Kingfisher

Woodpeckers and Allies

- ☐ Lewis's Woodpecker
- ☐ Red-headed Woodpecker *
- ☐ Acorn Woodpecker
- ☐ Gila Woodpecker
- ☐ Williamson's Sapsucker
- ☐ Yellow-bellied Sapsucker
- ☐ Red-naped Sapsucker
- ☐ Red-breasted Sapsucker
- ☐ Ladder-backed Woodpecker
- ☐ Nuttall's Woodpecker
- ☐ Downy Woodpecker
- ☐ Hairy Woodpecker
- ☐ White-headed Woodpecker
- ☐ Black-backed Woodpecker
- ☐ Northern Flicker
- ☐ Gilded Flicker
- ☐ Pileated Woodpecker

Caracaras and Falcons

- ☐ Crested Caracara *PV
- ☐ Eurasian Kestrel *P
- ☐ American Kestrel
- ☐ Merlin
- ☐ Gyrfalcon *
- ☐ Peregrine Falcon
- ☐ Prairie Falcon

Lories, Parakeets, Macaws, and Parrots

- ☐ Red-crowned Parrot I

Tyrant Flycatchers

- ☐ Olive-sided Flycatcher
- ☐ Greater Pewee *
- ☐ Western Wood-Pewee
- ☐ Eastern Wood-Pewee *PA
- ☐ Yellow-bellied Flycatcher *
- ☐ Alder Flycatcher *
- ☐ Willow Flycatcher
- ☐ Least Flycatcher
- ☐ Hammond's Flycatcher
- ☐ Gray Flycatcher
- ☐ Dusky Flycatcher
- ☐ Pacific-slope Flycatcher
- ☐ Cordilleran Flycatcher
- ☐ Black Phoebe
- ☐ Eastern Phoebe
- ☐ Say's Phoebe
- ☐ Vermilion Flycatcher
- ☐ Dusky-capped Flycatcher *
- ☐ Ash-throated Flycatcher
- ☐ Nutting's Flycatcher *PVA
- ☐ Great Crested Flycatcher *
- ☐ Brown-crested Flycatcher
- ☐ Sulphur-bellied Flycatcher *PV
- ☐ Tropical Kingbird
- ☐ Couch's Kingbird *PA
- ☐ Cassin's Kingbird
- ☐ Thick-billed Kingbird *PVA
- ☐ Western Kingbird
- ☐ Eastern Kingbird
- ☐ Scissor-tailed Flycatcher
- ☐ Fork-tailed Flycatcher *P

Shrikes

- ☐ Brown Shrike *P
- ☐ Loggerhead Shrike
- ☐ Northern Shrike

Vireos

- ☐ White-eyed Vireo *PA
- ☐ Bell's Vireo
- ☐ Gray Vireo
- ☐ Yellow-throated Vireo
- ☐ Plumbeous Vireo
- ☐ Cassin's Vireo
- ☐ Blue-headed Vireo *
- ☐ Hutton's Vireo
- ☐ Warbling Vireo
- ☐ Philadelphia Vireo
- ☐ Red-eyed Vireo
- ☐ Yellow-green Vireo

Crows and Jays

- ☐ Gray Jay
- ☐ Pinyon Jay
- ☐ Steller's Jay
- ☐ Blue Jay *
- ☐ Island Scrub-Jay
- ☐ Western Scrub-Jay
- ☐ Clark's Nutcracker
- ☐ Black-billed Magpie
- ☐ Yellow-billed Magpie
- ☐ American Crow
- ☐ Common Raven

Larks

- ☐ Sky Lark *P
- ☐ Horned Lark

Swallows

- ☐ Purple Martin
- ☐ Tree Swallow
- ☐ Violet-green Swallow
- ☐ Northern Rough-winged Swallow
- ☐ Bank Swallow
- ☐ Cliff Swallow
- ☐ Cave Swallow *P
- ☐ Barn Swallow

Chickadees and Titmice

- ☐ Black-capped Chickadee
- ☐ Mountain Chickadee
- ☐ Chestnut-backed Chickadee

- ☐ Oak Titmouse
- ☐ Juniper Titmouse

Penduline Tits and Verdins

- ☐ Verdin

Long-tailed Tits and Bushtits

- ☐ Bushtit

Nuthatches

- ☐ Red-breasted Nuthatch
- ☐ White-breasted Nuthatch
- ☐ Pygmy Nuthatch

Creepers

- ☐ Brown Creeper

Wrens

- ☐ Rock Wren
- ☐ Canyon Wren
- ☐ House Wren
- ☐ Pacific Wren
- ☐ Winter Wren *PA
- ☐ Sedge Wren *PA
- ☐ Marsh Wren
- ☐ Bewick's Wren
- ☐ Cactus Wren

Gnatcatchers and Gnatwrens

- ☐ Blue-gray Gnatcatcher
- ☐ California Gnatcatcher
- ☐ Black-tailed Gnatcatcher

Dippers

- ☐ American Dipper

Kinglets

- ☐ Golden-crowned Kinglet
- ☐ Ruby-crowned Kinglet

Leaf Warblers

- ☐ Dusky Warbler *
- ☐ Arctic/Kamchatka Leaf Warbler *P

Sylviid Warblers

- ☐ Wrentit

Grasshopper-Warblers

- ☐ Lanceolated Warbler *P

Old World Flycatchers

- ☐ Bluethroat *P
- ☐ Red-flanked Bluetail *P
- ☐ Taiga Flycatcher *P
- ☐ Northern Wheatear *
- ☐ Stonechat *P

Thrushes

- ☐ Western Bluebird
- ☐ Mountain Bluebird
- ☐ Townsend's Solitaire
- ☐ Veery *P
- ☐ Gray-cheeked Thrush *
- ☐ Swainson's Thrush
- ☐ Hermit Thrush
- ☐ Wood Thrush *
- ☐ Eyebrowed Thrush *PV
- ☐ Rufous-backed Robin *P
- ☐ American Robin
- ☐ Varied Thrush

Mockingbirds and Thrashers

- ☐ Gray Catbird
- ☐ Curve-billed Thrasher *
- ☐ Brown Thrasher
- ☐ Bendire's Thrasher
- ☐ California Thrasher
- ☐ Le Conte's Thrasher
- ☐ Crissal Thrasher
- ☐ Sage Thrasher
- ☐ Northern Mockingbird

Starlings

- ☐ European Starling I

Wagtails and Pipits

- ☐ Eastern Yellow Wagtail *P
- ☐ Gray Wagtail *P
- ☐ White Wagtail *P
- ☐ Olive-backed Pipit *P
- ☐ Red-throated Pipit
- ☐ American Pipit
- ☐ Sprague's Pipit

Waxwings

- ☐ Bohemian Waxwing
- ☐ Cedar Waxwing

Silky-flycatchers

- ☐ Phainopepla

Longspurs and Snow Buntings

- ☐ Lapland Longspur
- ☐ Chestnut-collared Longspur
- ☐ Smith's Longspur *PV
- ☐ McCown's Longspur
- ☐ Snow Bunting *

Wood-Warblers

- ☐ Ovenbird
- ☐ Worm-eating Warbler *
- ☐ Louisiana Waterthrush *
- ☐ Northern Waterthrush
- ☐ Golden-winged Warbler *
- ☐ Blue-winged Warbler *
- ☐ Black-and-white Warbler
- ☐ Prothonotary Warbler
- ☐ Tennessee Warbler
- ☐ Orange-crowned Warbler
- ☐ Lucy's Warbler
- ☐ Nashville Warbler
- ☐ Virginia's Warbler
- ☐ Connecticut Warbler *
- ☐ MacGillivray's Warbler
- ☐ Mourning Warbler *
- ☐ Kentucky Warbler
- ☐ Common Yellowthroat
- ☐ Hooded Warbler
- ☐ American Redstart
- ☐ Cape May Warbler *
- ☐ Cerulean Warbler *
- ☐ Northern Parula
- ☐ Magnolia Warbler
- ☐ Bay-breasted Warbler
- ☐ Blackburnian Warbler
- ☐ Yellow Warbler
- ☐ Chestnut-sided Warbler
- ☐ Blackpoll Warbler
- ☐ Black-throated Blue Warbler
- ☐ Palm Warbler
- ☐ Pine Warbler
- ☐ Yellow-rumped Warbler
- ☐ Yellow-throated Warbler
- ☐ Prairie Warbler
- ☐ Grace's Warbler *
- ☐ Black-throated Gray Warbler
- ☐ Townsend's Warbler
- ☐ Hermit Warbler

- ☐ Golden-cheeked Warbler *
- ☐ Black-throated Green Warbler
- ☐ Canada Warbler
- ☐ Wilson's Warbler
- ☐ Red-faced Warbler *
- ☐ Painted Redstart
- ☐ Yellow-breasted Chat

Emberizids

- ☐ Green-tailed Towhee
- ☐ Spotted Towhee
- ☐ Rufous-crowned Sparrow
- ☐ California Towhee
- ☐ Abert's Towhee
- ☐ Cassin's Sparrow *
- ☐ American Tree Sparrow
- ☐ Chipping Sparrow
- ☐ Clay-colored Sparrow
- ☐ Brewer's Sparrow
- ☐ Field Sparrow *[P]
- ☐ Black-chinned Sparrow
- ☐ Vesper Sparrow
- ☐ Lark Sparrow
- ☐ Black-throated Sparrow
- ☐ Sagebrush Sparrow
- ☐ Bell's Sparrow
- ☐ Lark Bunting
- ☐ Savannah Sparrow
- ☐ Grasshopper Sparrow
- ☐ Baird's Sparrow *
- ☐ Le Conte's Sparrow *
- ☐ Nelson's Sparrow
- ☐ Fox Sparrow
- ☐ Song Sparrow
- ☐ Lincoln's Sparrow
- ☐ Swamp Sparrow
- ☐ White-throated Sparrow
- ☐ Harris's Sparrow
- ☐ White-crowned Sparrow
- ☐ Golden-crowned Sparrow
- ☐ Dark-eyed Junco
- ☐ Little Bunting *[P]
- ☐ Rustic Bunting *[P]

Cardinals and Allies

- ☐ Hepatic Tanager
- ☐ Summer Tanager
- ☐ Scarlet Tanager
- ☐ Western Tanager
- ☐ Northern Cardinal
- ☐ Pyrrhuloxia *[P]
- ☐ Rose-breasted Grosbeak
- ☐ Black-headed Grosbeak
- ☐ Blue Grosbeak
- ☐ Lazuli Bunting
- ☐ Indigo Bunting
- ☐ Varied Bunting *
- ☐ Painted Bunting
- ☐ Dickcissel

Blackbirds

- ☐ Bobolink
- ☐ Red-winged Blackbird
- ☐ Tricolored Blackbird
- ☐ Western Meadowlark
- ☐ Yellow-headed Blackbird
- ☐ Rusty Blackbird *
- ☐ Brewer's Blackbird
- ☐ Common Grackle *
- ☐ Great-tailed Grackle
- ☐ Bronzed Cowbird
- ☐ Brown-headed Cowbird
- ☐ Orchard Oriole
- ☐ Hooded Oriole
- ☐ Streak-backed Oriole *
- ☐ Bullock's Oriole
- ☐ Baltimore Oriole
- ☐ Scott's Oriole

Fringilline and Cardueline Finches and Allies

- ☐ Brambling *[PV]
- ☐ Gray-crowned Rosy-Finch
- ☐ Black Rosy-Finch *
- ☐ Pine Grosbeak
- ☐ Common Rosefinch *[P]
- ☐ House Finch
- ☐ Purple Finch
- ☐ Cassin's Finch
- ☐ Red Crossbill
- ☐ White-winged Crossbill *[S]
- ☐ Common Redpoll *
- ☐ Pine Siskin
- ☐ Lesser Goldfinch
- ☐ Lawrence's Goldfinch
- ☐ American Goldfinch
- ☐ Evening Grosbeak

Old World Sparrows

- ☐ House Sparrow [I]

Waxbills and Allies

- ☐ Scaly-breasted Munia [I]

Species Index

U

V

W

X

Y

Z

Colophon

The text of this book is set in 8/11.5 pt *Excelsior*, designed by Chauncey H. Griffith in 1931 as part of Merganthaler Linotype's "Legibility Group" of newspaper typefaces.

The heads are set in *Clarendon Light*, designed by Hermann Eidenbenz in 1953 after Robert Besley's *Clarendon* designs originally released in 1845.

The captions are set in *Tangent Thin*, designed in 2006 by James Montalbano of Terminal Design

All production files were prepared on Macintosh computers.

The pages were composed in Adobe Indesign.

It was printed and bound in China.

Print production was managed by René Nedelkoff and the Four Colour Printing Group.

The paper is 115 gsm GE matte art.

It was edited by Rick Wright, Paul Hess, and George Scott.

It was designed by Charles Nix.

Quick Index

See the Species Index for a complete listing of all the birds in the *ABA Field Guide to Birds of California*.